Human Flourishing in the Age of Digital Capitalism

ALSO AVAILABLE FROM BLOOMSBURY

Virtue Ethics and Contemporary Aristotelianism: Modernity, Conflict and Politics, edited by Andrius Bielskis, Eleni Leontsini and Kelvin Knight

Machines Against Measures, Irene Sotiropoulou

Great Philosophical Objections to Artificial Intelligence: The History and Legacy of the AI Wars, Eric Dietrich, Chris Fields, John P. Sullins, Bram Van Heuveln and Robin Zebrowski

Distracted from Meaning: A Philosophy of Smartphones, Tiger C. Roholt

Human Flourishing in the Age of Digital Capitalism: AI, Automation and Alienation

Editor: Andrius Bielskis

BLOOMSBURY ACADEMIC
LONDON • NEW YORK • OXFORD • NEW DELHI • SYDNEY

BLOOMSBURY ACADEMIC
Bloomsbury Publishing Plc
50 Bedford Square, London, WC1B 3DP, UK
1385 Broadway, New York, NY 10018, USA
29 Earlsfort Terrace, Dublin 2, Ireland

BLOOMSBURY, BLOOMSBURY ACADEMIC and the Diana logo
are trademarks of Bloomsbury Publishing Plc

First published in Great Britain 2025

Copyright © Andrius Bielskis and Contributors, 2025

Andrius Bielskis and Contributors have asserted their right under the Copyright, Designs and Patents Act, 1988, to be identified as Authors of this work.

For legal purposes the Acknowledgements on p. xiv constitute
an extension of this copyright page.

Cover design by Chris Bromley
Cover image: The Knifegrinder or Principle of Glittering by Kazimir Malevich, 1913.
Yale University Art Gallery. (Wikimedia Commons / Public Domain)

All rights reserved. No part of this publication may be: i) reproduced or transmitted in any form, electronic or mechanical, including photocopying, recording or by means of any information storage or retrieval system without prior permission in writing from the publishers; or ii) used or reproduced in any way for the training, development or operation of artificial intelligence (AI) technologies, including generative AI technologies. The rights holders expressly reserve this publication from the text and data mining exception as per Article 4(3) of the Digital Single Market Directive (EU) 2019/790.

Bloomsbury Publishing Plc does not have any control over, or responsibility for, any third-party websites referred to or in this book. All internet addresses given in this book were correct at the time of going to press. The author and publisher regret any inconvenience caused if addresses have changed or sites have ceased to exist, but can accept no responsibility for any such changes.

A catalogue record for this book is available from the British Library.

A catalog record for this book is available from the Library of Congress.

ISBN: HB: 978-1-3505-1072-2
PB: 978-1-3505-1071-5
ePDF: 978-1-3505-1074-6
eBook: 978-1-3505-1073-9

Typeset by Integra Software Services Pvt. Ltd.
Printed and bound in Great Britain

For product safety related questions contact productsafety@bloomsbury.com.

To find out more about our authors and books visit www.bloomsbury.com
and sign up for our newsletters.

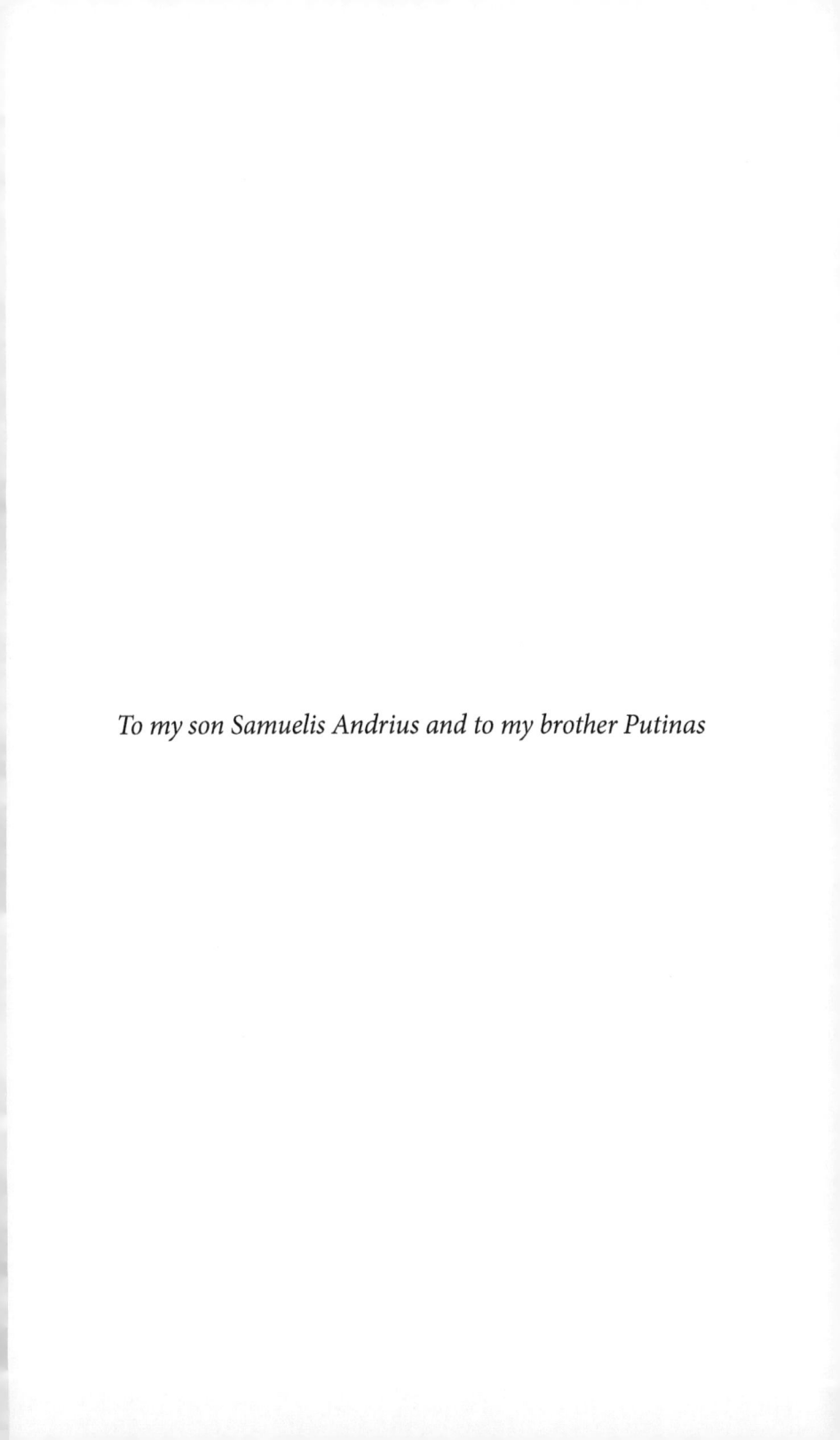

To my son Samuelis Andrius and to my brother Putinas

Contents

Notes on Contributors ix
Acknowledgements xiv

Introduction: Why We Need Aristotle and Marx Together *Andrius Bielskis* 1

1. On Sheep and Self-Moving Tools: The Material Conditions for Human Flourishing *Andrius Bielskis* 11

2. *Technē* in the Conflicts of Modernity: A MacIntyrean Approach to Technology *Kelvin Knight and Joe Simpson* 41

3. Algorithmic Management: The Corrupting Power of Technology *Pablo García Ruiz* 63

4. 'Mild Preparations': Work, Practices and the Internal Good of Recognition *Matthew Sinnicks, Efuntomi Wosu and Craig Reeves* 89

5. A Note on Marx, Alienation and Technology *Ruth Porter Groff* 109

6. Artificial Intelligence, Alienation and the Existential Conditions of Human Flourishing *Jeff Noonan* 129

7   Marxism and the Idea of a Fully Automated Machine
    Society: Science Fiction Utopia or Dystopian
    Nightmare? *Tony Burns* 159

8   Automation and the Good Life: Technological
    Enslavement, Technological Liberation or
    Technology Transformed? *Egidijus Mardosas* 187

Index 213

Contributors

Andrius Bielskis is Director of the Centre for Aristotelian Studies and Critical Theory at Mykolas Romeris University, Lithuania, and Professor of Philosophy at Kaunas University of Technology, Lithuania. He is the author of several books including *Towards a Postmodern Understanding of the Political* (2005), *The Unholy Sacrament* (in Lithuanian, 2014), *On the Meaning of Philosophy and Art* (in Lithuanian, 2015), *Existence, Meaning, Excellence* (2017), and is the co-editor of *Virtue Ethics and Contemporary Aristotelianism* (Bloomsbury, 2020), *Virtue and Economy* (2015), *Debating with the Lithuanian New Left: Terry Eagleton, Joel Bakan, Alex Demirovic, Ulrich Brand* (2014) and *Democracy without Labour Movement?* (in Lithuanian, 2009) and has published scholarly papers in journals such as *Capital and Class*, *Journal of Philosophy of Education* and *Critique: Journal of Socialist Thought*. He was an International Onassis Fellow at the University of Athens, Greece, in 2017–18, pursuing research on the critique of natural inequalities in Aristotle's *Politics*. Andrius is the Founder and Director of DEMOS Institute of Critical Thought. He has led and completed a research project called 'Human Flourishing and Non-Alienated Labour in the Era of Automation' (2021–4) funded by the Research Council of Lithuania. Currently, he is a 2024–5 Visiting Research Scholar at the Graduate Center of the City University of New York, USA, funded by the Baltic-American Freedom Foundation (BAFF).

Tony Burns is a Professor Emeritus of Political Theory at the University of Nottingham, UK, a Director of the Centre for the Study of Social and Global Justice (CSSFI) based in the UK, and International Research Fellow at the Centre for Aristotelian Studies and Critical Theory at Mykolas Romeris University, Lithuania. He is a historian of ideas, with a particular interest in the history of social and political theory. He has a related interest in political theory and science fiction, with a focus on the ethical and political implications of science and technology, as dealt with in works of art, especially literature. He has published widely on Aristotle, the Aristotelian political tradition, Marx, Hegel and Thomas Aquinas. He is the author of several monographs, including *Aristotle and Natural Law* (2011), of numerous scholarly papers in journals such as *Contemporary Political Theory* and *History of Political Thought*, and a co-editor of several volumes on the politics of recognition, literary utopias, the Hegel–Marx connection and Leo Strauss. He is currently working on a trilogy devoted to the theme of *Social Institutions and the Politics of Recognition in the History of Political Thought*. The first two volumes, *Social Institutions and the Politics of Recognition*, Volume 1: *From the Ancient Greeks to the Reformation* and Volume 2: *From the Reformation to the French Revolution*, were published in 2020. Volume 3, *From Hegel to the Present*, is to be published in 2026. Prof. Burns also took part in the research project 'Human Flourishing and Non-Alienated Labour in the Era of Automation' (2021–3) led by Prof. Bielskis.

Ruth Porter Groff is Professor of Political Science and Affiliated Professor of Philosophy at Saint Louis University, USA and International Research Fellow at the Centre for Aristotelian Studies and Critical Theory, Mykolas Romeris University, Lithuania. She is the author of *Ontology Revisited: Social and Political Philosophy* (2013) and *Critical Realism, Post-Positivism and the Possibility of Knowledge*

(2004). She is the editor of *Subject & Object: Frankfurt School Writings on Epistemology, Ontology and Metaphysics* (2014), as well as *Revitalizing Causality: Realism about Causality in Philosophy and Social Science* (2009) and co-editor, with John Greco, of *Powers and Capacities: The New Aristotelianism* (2013). She is looking forward to finishing a new book with Bloomsbury in the coming year, and is currently editing the *Routledge Handbook of Social Ontology*. She is founder and coordinator of the Critical Social Ontology Workshop, which holds an annual interdisciplinary, international, working conference on the nature of social phenomena.

Kelvin Knight is Senior Research Fellow at Mykolas Romeris University's Centre for Aristotelian Studies and Critical Theory, Lithuania, and was Director of CASEP (the Centre for Contemporary Aristotelian Studies in Ethics and Politics), when it was based at London Metropolitan University, UK, where he remains Reader in Ethics and Politics. He is author of *Aristotelian Philosophy: Ethics and Politics from Aristotle to MacIntyre* (2007), editor of *The MacIntyre Reader* (1998), co-editor and author of other works on contemporary Aristotelianism, and authoring a book on the history and philosophy of human rights.

Egidijus Mardosas is a Post-Doctoral Research Fellow in the Department of Philosophy at Vilnius University, Lithuania, and a Researcher Fellow at Mykolas Romeris University's Centre for Aristotelian Studies and Critical Theory, Lithuania. His research interests include contemporary Aristotelianism, Marxism, Critical Theory and the Anthropocene. He is the author of *Revolutionary Aristotelianism and Ideology: MacIntyre on Practical Reason and Virtue* (Bloomsbury, 2024). He is a member of New Directions in Humanities Research Network. Egidijus Mardosas also took part in the research project 'Human Flourishing and Non-Alienated Labour in the Era of Automation' (2021–4) led by Prof. Bielskis.

Jeff Noonan is Professor of Philosophy at the University of Windsor, Canada. He is the author of *Critical Humanism and the Politics of Difference* (2003), *Democratic Society and Human Needs* (2006), *Materialist Ethics and Life-Value* (2012), *Embodiment and the Meaning of Life* (2018), *The Troubles with Democracy* (2019) and *Embodied Humanism: Towards Sensuousness and Solidarity* (2022). He has published dozens of peer reviewed articles in philosophy, political theory and interdisciplinary journals as well as numerous book chapters. He also writes regularly for alternative and progressive websites in Canada and abroad and maintains an active blog at www.jeffnoonan.org.

Craig Reeves is Lecturer in Law at Birkbeck College, UK. His research focuses on issues in moral philosophy, critical theory, and philosophy of law, and his work has appeared in scholarly journals, such as *Res Publica*, *Social and Legal Studies*, *Journal of Critical Realism* and *Law and Critique*.

Pablo García Ruiz is Associate Professor of Sociology at the University of Zaragoza, Spain. He is currently president of the Aragon Association of Sociology. His current research deals with the impact of technology on the organization of work. He is the author of numerous studies, including the books *Sociologia Relacional. Una lectura de la sociedad emergente* (2021); *Sociology of Organizations* (co-authored with Antonio Lucas, 2013); *Repensar el consumo* (2009) and *Poder y Sociedad. La sociología política de Talcott Parsons* (1993). His most recent articles include 'Artificial Intelligence Ethics in Business', *Frontiers in Psychology* (2023); 'Ratings and Rankings: the Consumption–Work link in the Platform Economy' (*Revista Española de Sociología*, 2023); 'Measuring Happiness for Social Policy Evaluation: A Multidimensional Index of Happiness' (*Sociological Spectrum*, 2023) and 'The Digital Transformation of Work. A Relational

View' (*BEER*, 2021). He was a keynote speaker at the 2023 Annual Meeting of ISME, the International Society for MacIntyrean Enquiry, where he delivered a lecture entitled 'Can Work Be Meaningful under Algorithmic Management?'

Joe Simpson started his career in the voluntary sector before working in television for over twenty years (whilst also being active in politics). He then established a major public service leadership organization in the United Kingdom, leading it until his retirement in 2022. He is now studying for a PhD, exploring the political work of Alasdair MacIntyre (whom he initially studied over fifty years ago).

Matthew Sinnicks is Associate Professor at Southampton Business School in the University of Southampton, UK. His research interests include flourishing and alienation in the workplace, the ethical quality of market society, and the work of Alasdair MacIntyre. His work has appeared in journals such as *Business Ethics Quarterly*, *Journal of Business Ethics* and *Business & Society*.

Efuntomi Wosu is a PhD student in the Department of Leadership, Organisations and Behaviour, at Henley Business School in the University of Reading, UK. Her research focuses on leadership virtue character and development, with a specific interest in applying MacIntyre's virtue ethics to leadership virtue development, particularly the role of practical wisdom and moral courage in human flourishing.

Acknowledgements

This book is the result of a three-year research project, 'Human Flourishing and Non-Alienated Labour in the Age of Automation', funded by a grant (No. S-MIP-21-48) from the Research Council of Lithuania. I am grateful to the Council for their support and for the opportunity to explore technological advancement, particularly AI-driven automation, from the perspective of normative critical theory and the intersection of Aristotelianism and Marxism.

Introduction

Why We Need Aristotle and Marx Together

Andrius Bielskis

The edited volume you have in your hands is the result of a three-year research project conducted by several members of the Centre for Aristotelian Studies and Critical Theory (CASCT) in Vilnius. Established in 2018, the Centre aims to advance Aristotelian research and engage contemporary Aristotelianism in philosophical conversation with critical theory. Critical theory, in this context, is understood in the broadest possible sense: both as a critique of the dominant social and political order and as an attempt to theorize an emancipated and just society. The philosophical premise of this book lies in our belief that rapid technological advancement should be theorized through the intersection between contemporary appropriations of Aristotle and Marxist critical theory.

The image on the cover of the book is no accident, even though the decision to use it – thanks to Simon Willems – was made after the manuscript had been completed and submitted to the publisher. The 1912 painting *The Knifegrinder* by Ukrainian avant-garde artist Kazimir Malevich (in Russian, Точильщик) depicts a worker in a workshop in a futuristic, cubist style. This cover reflects the spirit of the collection well: it emphasizes workers as practitioners, the true creators of use values, values that cannot be generated without tools and technological advancement. This theme runs throughout the essays in the volume. One of the book's central arguments is that Artificial Intelligence (AI) is yet another highly sophisticated and evolving tool.

There can be no doubt that AI and automation will dramatically change our societies. Public debates on AI in particular have intensified since the launch of OpenAI's ChatGPT. Reactions have varied – from the uncritical adoration of AI and its potential to dramatically transform social life, to speculation on existential threats and even the very survival of humanity. Elon Musk, for example, has warned that AI poses enormous risks and may even destroy humanity, suggesting that its development should be put on hold. His own AI startup, ironically, is now accumulating billions of dollars in investments in order to enter the capitalist AI arms race, seeking its far-reaching application in our daily lives.

These debates are also increasingly intense in the theoretical literature, albeit in their more sophisticated forms. Yet the deliberations of academia also reflect the hopes and fears of the general public. On the one hand, there is a growing body of literature which, following Martin Heidegger's 'The Question Concerning Technology' (1954), sees technological advancement, including the development of AI, in negative terms as a huge threat. Technopessimists' speculations on technology follow, or rather reflect, the long tradition of dystopian literature – Yevgeny Zamyatin's *We*, Aldous Huxley's *Brave New World*, George Orwell's *1984*, etc. – which, among other things, is discussed by Tony Burns in his excellent chapter in this book. For some of these theorists, the development of AI, especially its all-powerful future form of artificial general intelligence (AGI), must be either paused or controlled. If humanity creates superintelligent machines that are smarter than human beings, then not only will it be extremely difficult to control them, but, as Nick Bostrom has argued, AI will also pose fundamental existential risks, including the possible destruction of humanity.

Others, on the contrary, welcome technological progress. Techno-optimists (or technophiles, as Amy Wendling called them in *Marx on Technology and Alienation* (2009)) echo the techno-utopian literature of Herbert George Wells and Edward Bellamy in parallel, both of whom are discussed by Tony Burns and Egidijus Mardosas in their chapters. They celebrate technological achievements, arguing that AI and automation have the potential to produce conditions for future societies which, as much as possible, will free us from the sphere of necessity and the need to work. Nick Srnicek and Alex Williams's *Inventing the Future: Postcapitalism and a World without Work* (2015), Paul Mason's *Postcapitalism* (2015) and Aaron Bastani's *Fully Automated Luxury Communism* (2019) are perhaps the best examples of this techno-optimist automated future, and their works are also critically debated by Bielskis and Mardosas in their respective chapters.

The aim of this book is to navigate between these two philosophical positions – technophobe and technophile – by analysing the actual forms of technology that are present in today's digital capitalism and by reflecting on possible alternative visions of technology. The key question, therefore, is how to reframe reflections about technology, including AI, without being either blatantly optimistic or overtly pessimistic. We need to ask uncomfortable questions: Why can't we control the development of AI? Does a democratic society have a stake in what is going on within giant AI-producing corporations? What are the underlying interests behind the AI industry? Perhaps most importantly: What impact do existing forms of technology, automation and AI have on human flourishing?

This book is written from the point of view (either explicitly or implicitly, as in the case of Jeff Noonan's chapter) that Aristotle (and his appropriation by Alasdair MacIntyre) and Karl Marx together provide the philosophical and theoretical resources necessary to reflect on these challenging issues.

Aristotle is important for several reasons. First, it was Aristotle whose concept of *automata*, of self-moving tools, was the predecessor of our use of 'automation'. In the first book of *Politics*, Aristotle, against his own better judgement, notoriously argues that there are 'natural slaves' – people who are slaves not by circumstances, but by nature. However, as if contradicting his own claims, Aristotle then suggests that if humans had tools that could move 'of their own motion', then we would not need despotic relations with slaves and subordinates. Today, as the first chapter argues, we are surrounded by these automated tools.

At the same time, Aristotle is significant because he developed a compelling normative conception of happiness – *eudaimonia*, which is best translated as 'human flourishing'. At the centre of this conception is the claim that a good human life is a life of activity; thus, a passive life cannot be a happy one. A flourishing life is one in which we employ our essential faculties: first and foremost, the faculty of reason (*logos*), as the *ergon* (work/function) of the human form of life. Thus, a flourishing life is one in which we properly employ our rational, creative, aesthetic and moral powers. For such a life, virtues or moral excellence/s (*aretē*) of character, such as justice, courage, wisdom and self-control, are also necessary. Alasdair MacIntyre's philosophical project of *After Virtue* (1981), arguably the most powerful contemporary appropriation of Aristotle, has inspired many of the authors of this book (notably Kelvin Knight and Joe Simpson, Matthew Sinnicks, Efuntomi Wosu, Craig Reeves, Pablo García Ruiz and Andrius Bielskis).

Given that AI is penetrating all areas of our lives, unemployment caused by technological progress will increase. Thus, a very important question needs to be asked: What work do we, as a society, want to automate? Moreover, what will we do with our lives when, as John Maynard Keynes famously put it, economic problems are solved while mankind is deprived of its traditional purpose? Should we not 'expect a general nervous breakdown' (as discussed in the chapter by Matthew Sinnicks, Efuntomi Wosu and Craig Reeves)? In other words, if we accept the Aristotelian premise that human flourishing means living an active, creative life engaged in meaningful activities and (MacIntyrean) practices that develop and expand our human capacities and essential powers, then it is important to ask a normative question: What ought to be automated and what should not?

On the other hand, Karl Marx is important because of his historical materialism and his sociological realism. Marx's famous 1859 thesis containing his materialist understanding of history is discussed in the first chapter, and its importance for our analysis of societal changes today is underlined. The key to this conception is the distinction between the forces of production and the relations of production (or property relations). Marx argues that as humanity develops, the tools necessary for our existence also develop, as do our productive forces (technologies, know-how and the means of production). People's needs also change and develop over the course of history. Over time, technological progress and the accumulation of non-perishable wealth make societies richer: there is no longer a need to reinvent the bicycle or the computer. Yet for a flourishing life – and here Aristotle and Marx agree – we need free time so that we can create and enjoy the arts, engage in philosophical reflections and conduct other meaningful practices. Therefore, Marx's historical materialism presupposes that freedom is achieved when people are freed, as much as possible, from the sphere of necessity.

With the development of tools, the rise of automation and now AI (which, as the first chapter argues, is another sophisticated tool), we can create wealth much more easily than we could in the past. However, therein lies the paradox: the tools and the forces of production have developed greatly, and societies *in toto* have become richer, but do we work fewer hours to meet our needs? In 1930, Keynes argued that his grandchildren's generation would work 15 hours a week, and that existing technological progress would allow us to meet our needs by working just 3 hours per day. Technological progress has taken place, yet the length of the working day has not changed since the mid-1940s. Hence the importance of the Marx-inspired critique of the existing political economy, including the political economy of the AI industry and current forms of automation. In other words, we need to question existing forms of property relations, including those within the AI industry: Who own the main AI-producing companies? How do they function, and what kind of labour processes exist? As a democratic society, we have the right to know where AI is heading and to participate in the processes surrounding it.

These are just some of the questions discussed in this volume, but it would be wrong to claim that its authors comprehensively answer them. Nonetheless, this is the direction in which we need to travel. As such, the chapters of this book are not structured in any order of priority. While they can certainly be read separately, the first chapter is perhaps the most programmatic and covers the majority of the topics discussed in this introduction. Despite the free-standing nature of its chapters, there are two rough conceptual sections to this work which, of course, are intertwined.

The first four chapters are more Aristotelian–MacIntyrean in their nature. Written from the point of view of the distinction between practices and institutions and drawing on Harry Braverman's critique of Taylorist managerialism aimed at the deskilling of workers, the second chapter, by Kelvin Knight and Joe Simpson, is the most MacIntyrean. In it, the authors argue that technology and technological innovation have been advanced first and foremost by workers themselves – that is, by workers as practitioners who used their practical rationalities to improve practices they were involved in. On the other hand, Pablo García Ruiz, while engaging with MacIntyre's critique of managers, asks whether and to what extent algorithmic management manifests the traits that MacIntyre attributes to professional management. The third chapter also discusses new forms of alienation generated by algorithmic management, which is increasingly replacing human managers. Following the Aristotelian premise of human flourishing as an activity, the chapter argues that work is a crucial element for human flourishing and asks what algorithmic management does to it.

Chapter 4 engages with post-work and anti-work literature, and positions MacIntyre's Aristotelianism along the lines of Keynes's 'mild preparation' for a future of leisure without breakdown which, according to Matthew Sinnicks, Efuntomi Wosu and Craig Reeves, would require our capacity for enjoyment and the recognition of those who engage in practices. Recognition, according to the authors, is an 'internal good' of a (MacIntyrean) practice. Of course, the issue of whether recognition can be seen as an internal good of a practice is a contentious one. Recognition, *sensu stricto*, is an external good, as the authors of the chapter acknowledge. This is so because the very act of recognition comes from another person (therefore it is external; its 'source' lies outside the activity itself). Moreover, recognition is a variant of status or, to be more precise, status is a variant of recognition, which is an external good. However, it is indeed true that recognition is the locus where internal and external goods meet, as the authors correctly claim. In a way, arguments made about management as a 'domain-relative practice' apply here as well: we can say that recognition is a 'domain-relative good'.

Chapters 5, 6, 7 and 8 deal more with aspects of Marxism, although they (especially Chapters 5 and 8) are also informed by Aristotelianism. Ruth Groff provides an Aristotelian reading of Marx's conception of alienation, and shows the continuity of the alienation argument from the *Paris Manuscripts* through to *Capital*. Following Marcuse and Adorno's insights, she argues that technology in capitalism has a specific capitalist form, and that each technology (or technological device) is contradictory: it is a result of capitalist alienation, yet still, as a specific use value, can contribute to human flourishing. Jeff Noonan's chapter explains why we cannot understand human intelligence if we abstract its functioning from our embodied lives. Intelligence is an expression of human life, and unless and until AI systems become consciously and bodily alive, they will lack the interests and purposes that both characterize the exercise of human intelligence and constitute its unique value. Chapter 6 also argues that the techno-utopian argument that AI will soon exhibit 'superintelligence' is and should be understood as the expression of alienation and our alienated understanding of human intelligence.

The final two chapters delve into utopian and dystopian literary imaginations and discuss further alienating aspects of technology in capitalism. Tony Burns questions the assumptions upon which the dystopian critique of Marx's vision of a fully automated society is based. Engaging with, among other things, early Bolshevik debates on the nature of technology in socialism, especially Lenin's technocracy and its critique by Alexander Bogdanov, Burns draws the conclusion that the critique of Marx by dystopian authors is not fully applicable to Marx himself, and that these early twentieth-century debates on the role of technology in a good society have great relevance today. Egidijus Mardosas's closing chapter, starting from Edward Bellamy and William Morris's literary works, goes on to argue that technoptimist and technopessimist positions remain one-sided; thus, we need a third position. Such a position would accept the importance of technology in making our lives better but would reject the alienating forms of technology developed under capitalism.

In short: Aristotle and Marx together, indeed! We need a robust, non-subjectivist account of human flourishing; a normative foundation on which to judge technological advancement, including AI-driven automation; and a no-bullshit materialist critique of the many alienating forms of technology, with a healthy dose of Marxist sociology and political economy thrown in for good measure. If this volume has moved the discourse even slightly toward this end, then it can already be considered a success.

1

On Sheep and Self-Moving Tools

The Material Conditions for Human Flourishing

Andrius Bielskis

Introduction

We live in dramatic times that bear witness to wars and geopolitical instability, the climate crisis and the unprecedented technological advancement of Artificial Intelligence (AI)-driven automation. The launch of ChatGPT by OpenAI in 2022 accelerated discussions that have been ongoing for some time: the exponential growth of investment in the AI industry by a small number of tech giants, increasing competition between China and the USA, and exaggerated public speculation on the far-reaching consequences of AI on human life. Soon after ChatGPT was launched, billionaire Elon Musk warned that AI poses risks and may destroy humanity, and that therefore its development should be put on hold. Nonetheless, his own AI startup, xAI, is now accumulating billions of dollars in investments in order to join the capitalist race for the tool which, he believes, will one day make human labour obsolete. Herein lies the predicament of our time. Born out of the military industry and publicly funded in the 1950s and 1960s, the privately owned AI industry appropriated previously state-funded research and knowledge during the neoliberal era to become fully commodified and controlled by a dozen tech corporations. Now, the reverse is happening. Defence ministries and police departments, through notorious public–private partnership schemes, commission Google to employ thousands of ghost workers to sort through hours of drone videos or to face-tag and train facial recognition algorithms.[1] The micro-work that is so essential for the AI industry is being done by an invisible army of workers all over the world. The levels of alienation involved in this form of micro-work are unprecedented even when compared to factory work in the nineteenth century. This work is completely fragmented and anonymous, as workers are separated from one another and have no understanding either of how the tasks that they perform contribute to the final product or even what this product is.

This is then the horizon of the unfortunate neoliberal political economy of digital capitalism, which requires renewed analysis. Automated tools have reached an unprecedented level of sophistication, yet the existing property regime produces new forms of alienation and distress, while also increasing the risk of new forms of immiseration of the wageless existence. To advance this analysis, the intersection of two philosophical traditions will be theorized: Marxist historical materialism and Aristotelianism, in particular the Aristotelian account of human flourishing. Historical materialism provides us with a basis for a structural analysis of the forms of capitalist relations of production. Contemporary forms of automation have been made possible due to highly advanced technologies, which serve as sophisticated self-moving tools, instruments that are used in production and social reproduction. They constitute the enormous power of the current forces of production, which, in principle, should allow humans to produce the necessities of their lives much more easily and quickly than past tools. The new material condition (shaped by automated tools) creates new needs, yet the acceleration of technologies and instruments cannot be matched by the proliferation of our needs. Without engaging in old-fashioned speculation on needs versus wants, the philosophical questioning of our needs presupposes the question of what it is to live well. The premise of this chapter is that contemporary appropriations of Aristotle (especially by Alasdair MacIntyre) provide us with the possibility of arriving at a convincing answer to this question.

Historical Materialism

In the famous passage from *A Contribution to the Critique of Political Economy*, Marx ([1859] 1904) formulates his materialist conception of history. What follows in this section is an attempt to explain its central claim.

At the centre of Marx's conception is his belief that the analysis of the processes taking place in society must be based on an understanding of the material forces of production and the existing relations of production. Without understanding the contradictions of capitalist relations, we will not be able fully to understand the forms of social consciousness. This thesis is best elucidated through Marx's witty analogy: just as we do not judge a person based on what they think about themselves, we cannot judge changes and fundamental events in society by studying the forms of its consciousness. Rather, our investigations should start from the facticity of our material condition, and the manifestations of social consciousness – ideology in the broadest sense – must be understood against the background of the contradictions and existing conflicts of material life.

Similarly, in *The German Ideology*, written over a decade earlier, Marx and Engels argue that our enquiries should start from the fundamental fact that individuals exist, that humans have to produce the necessities of life to satisfy their needs, and that production takes place through their relationship with nature and involves cooperating with other people. In this way, humans produce not only the necessities of life but also their 'material life'. Work and labour (to be discussed in the next section) intervene between humans and nature, and out of the labour of wrestling with nature the means of subsistence are produced. Production in this sense is the distinguishing feature of being human. Furthermore, production as the creation of conditions for material life is also the condition for the development of human consciousness. Only by creating their own objectified world which surpasses a natural environment unaltered by intentional productive activity do humans develop consciousness. In this sense, Aristotle's claim that humans are political animals who possess reason (*logos*) is complementary to that of Marx. Human consciousness, powers of reasoning and language develop through the collective production and creation of the world as an objectified form of ourselves. At the centre of this collective process is a set of tools and instruments (*organa*, as Aristotle called them). Thus, as the production of living material conditions develops, so does society and its collective consciousness. Alongside the production of material conditions, the division of labour also increases. With the development of tools comes the growth of productive capacity and the complexity of the relations of production.

It is precisely between productive forces and productive relations that contradictions and conflicts eventually arise. At this point, Marx believed, a period of social instability and social revolution begins. The forces of production represent the totality of all collectively created existing tools and technologies, and the resulting productive capabilities. In Aristotle's age, people had shovels, pickaxes, hammers, handsaws and swords, while we have tractors, excavators, electric saws, airplanes, computers and now AI as the most powerful, albeit still developing, tool. Hence, our productive capability to build and produce things we need is thousands of times greater than that of Aristotle's contemporaries. Thus, if we, following Marx, assume that the development of the forces of production is at the heart of the historical development of humanity, then human history progresses in a specifically (narrow) materialist sense. New generations coming into the world find the pre-existing forces of production and all of the material culture created by previous generations. We do not need to invent the bicycle; it has already been invented. Tools evolve, and technological innovations are accumulated and passed down from generation to generation. At the same time, the entire material edifice of society – i.e. real estate and other non-perishable assets – is accumulated and passed on from generation to generation. In this way, from the point of view of material culture only, the forces of production and the generated wealth of mankind grow progressively, even if this claim does not mean that their historical development is immune to decline due to natural disasters, wars, crises and other calamities. Yet the growth of the forces of production, accumulated wealth and its benefits are unevenly distributed in societies, as their distribution depends on the relations of production existing at a given time. The latter are politically and legally established property relations – the relations of production.

The relations of production are social relations that are established and legally solidified in the process of the production of the necessities needed for our lives. The forces of production – the totality of tools and technologies – structure or determine the relations of production. Of course, this claim does not mean that there are immovable laws of history determining its development. In this sense, Karl Raimund Popper's (1961: vi–vii) thesis on the poverty of historicism – that the development of human history is influenced by the growth of knowledge and we cannot predict the future growth of scientific knowledge; thus, we cannot predict the future development of history and its laws – is broadly correct, and should not be opposed to the historical materialism defended here. The claim that the forces of production 'determine' the relations of production is best understood retrospectively by looking at the historical transformations of the past, rather than being used in our attempts to speculate or predict the future.[2] Nevertheless, a general trend can be formulated as follows: the improvement of tools and technologies and the growth of productive forces provide the material conditions for (but do not guarantee) the liberation of individuals from despotic natural and productive relations.[3]

The relations of production determine who does what in the production process, how it is organized, who and through what form of ownership the means of production are controlled, and who receives the surplus value created in production. If a group of individuals controls most of the country's means of production by some form of ownership, then that ownership gives them the opportunity to control the production process, to employ or otherwise use the labour of others, and to appropriate the product that is created. In this way, the ownership of the means of production (land, capital, tools, knowledge and money) gives their owner enormous power. This then creates a structural inequality between social classes in society – between those who control the means of production and the process of production, and those who work using these means to create a product that does not belong to them. This is how the social classes of rulers and ruled are formed, when the class controlling the means of production consolidates its dominance by legal and political means – that is, by using political power to consolidate its interests.

The totality of the relations of production and the forces of production constitutes a mode of production. The latter is not only a certain established order of dominant social relations but also a way of life. The mode of production, for Marx, is in a way akin to Aristotle's conception of *politeia* (constitution). For Aristotle, *politeia* is a communal way of life set in the institutional form of the political community. When people come into this world, they do not choose what socially established relationships they will enter into – these relationships are independent of people's will. The economic and political structure is the social horizon against which the consciousness of individuals who enter the world develops. This is the meaning of Marx's claim that the base – the economic foundation of society – shapes the expressions of the consciousness of individuals, which in turn is also shaped by the collective ideological superstructure of society. Thus, as Marx and Engels put it in *The German Ideology*, it is not consciousness that determines existence, but existence that determines consciousness.[4]

Leaving aside the different modes of production discussed by Marx and the forms of ownership related to them, the transformation from feudalism to capitalism will suffice to illustrate the conflict between the forces *and* relations of production. This transformation, being the best example of what Marx meant by social revolution, is paradigmatic. It allowed, as many interpreters and critics of Marx have argued, the concept of historical materialism to be formulated. Briefly, this conflict and the transformation it triggered can be described as follows. The form of property characteristic to feudalism had to be and was replaced by the privately owned form of property, as the former eventually became the fetter of the rapidly developing forces of production accelerating in, roughly, the sixteenth century. By the end of the sixteenth century, textile and other manufacturers were established in Europe and trade intensified.[5] This created a demand for, among other things, cotton, which became an incentive for the illegal process of enclosure in England beginning in the fifteenth century and gaining momentum in the sixteenth century. Enclosures became the first illegal privatization process in Europe, a process essential for the emergence of any form of capitalism.

The form of property inherent in feudalism meant that land was used in common. It was used not only by feudal lords but also by peasants tied to the land. In addition, land was not a commodity: feudal lords received it either as a gift for loyalty and service to the crown, or through inheritance. Similarly, part of the land controlled by feudal lords was given to peasants, who in return for the opportunity to use their plots of land also cultivated the feudal lord's land, while most of the produce went to the lord. The ownership of land by the feudal communities did not mean that everyone had the same claim to it and the product created in it, but it meant that the land was not the private property of a single landowner. When hit by the freezing cold, the peasants could freely pick wood from the land controlled by the feudal lord. Enclosure was the seizure of commonly used land. As E. P. Thompson argued in *The Making of the English Working Class*, this 'was a plain enough case of class robbery' (Thompson 1991: 237). Enclosure transformed peasants driven out from their land into workers who no longer had an independent means of subsistence. It also turned feudal landowners into the first capitalists who occupied land by force, declared the robbery of their private property, kicked out the peasants from the land and began rearing the sheep. Thus, in describing this process of illegal privatization, Marx quotes Thomas More's *Utopia*: 'sheep swallowed down the very men themselves' (cf. Marx 1990: 880). This condition for the development of capitalism became the process in which sheep 'ate' humans; it gave birth to the institution of private property essential for the capitalist mode of production.

Here we return to Marx's conception of social revolution in the 1859 preface. Social revolution arises from below, from the growth and development of the forces of production. It is a long, ongoing process. Thus, a revolution cannot be merely a *coup d'état* that replaces one political authority with another. The revolution begins in the economic base as the existing property relations begin to limit the development of the forces of production. Then, the resistance of the avant-garde social group to the stagnant productive relations gradually begins. The emerging new social class struggles for hegemony, and this struggle culminates in the consolidation of the dominance of its economic power through political means. In the case of the transformation from feudalism to capitalism, it was the political and economic victory of the bourgeoisie, the private owners of capital as the commodified means of production, over the land-owning aristocracy. The paradigmatic example of the political establishment of bourgeois class power was the so-called 'Glorious Revolution' of 1688 in England. This created a constitutional monarchy and, more importantly, politically established bourgeois private property rights by legalizing the seizure of the land that existed under common ownership.[6] Thus, by the eighteenth century, Adam Smith could assert 'the sacred rights of private property' and argue that these rights were essential for the development of capitalist markets (Smith 2007: 111).

Before we reflect on the importance of Marx's historical materialism, a clarification needs to be addressed. Historical materialism – as a theoretical–methodological approach emphasizing that the forces of production give rise to social revolution, which eventually explodes stagnant property relations – is suitable primarily, and perhaps only, for the historical transformation from feudalism to capitalism.

Thus, its explanatory power should not be overestimated. Cornelius Castoriadis, for example, argued that the historical transition of late Antiquity societies to early feudalism was a reverse process, when the far more technologically advanced Roman Empire was conquered by the less technologically developed Goth tribes. Castoriadis, along with many others, also rightly argued that history 'cannot be thought in accordance with the determinist schema [...] because it is the domain of creation' (Castoriadis 2005: 44–5). Leaving aside the fact that Marx and Engels mention this reverse transition in *The German Ideology*, the meaningful use of historical materialism in our analysis does not and cannot presuppose one-directional causality and determinism. The material contradictions within a given set of relations of production with certain tools and technologies can give birth to a great variety of different forms of consciousness (including, of course, false consciousness). Thus, in as much as human (collective and individual) actions are informed by thoughts about their material conditions, the possible responses to these contradictions will also vary. Nonetheless, what is undeniable is that our forces of production and accumulated wealth have grown and increased enormously in the course of human history.[7] It is against these conditions of accumulated wealth and the development of technologies that human flourishing should be conceptualized.

Flourishing and Non-Alienated Labour

Tools and AI as a Tool

Thus, given the discussion above, the question that we then need to pose is: What kind of labour or work do we *have* (that is, that which dominates in the world today) and what kind do we *want* to have (if at all), assuming the tools and technologies we have today? Moreover, how are we to understand the relationship between human flourishing and labour? Before sketching out possible answers to these questions, a working definition of a 'tool' is required. By a 'tool' we will mean any instrument that humans use to preserve their lives and meet their needs. Again, Marx's materialist insight on the transformation of human needs by tools is instructive here. Needs are open-ended in the sense of the claim that the satisfaction of one set of needs, 'the action of satisfying and the instrument of satisfaction which has been acquired, leads to new needs' (Marx and Engels 1988: 44). Tools encompass all of the instruments we use both in production and in the sphere of social reproduction (or, as Aristotle (1995: 1254a16) put it, for 'the purpose of action (*praxis*)', rather than solely being used in production (*poiesis*)): from hammers and sickles, computers and phones, to beds and tables. The function of a tool is to serve a particular human need, and as such, its form is tailored to meet that need (e.g. a spoon or a knife). Tools are functional; their quality is judged by their functionality. Tools, especially sophisticated ones, enhance human powers and often surpass human capabilities in specific domains. Consider a shovel compared to human hands. Using it surpasses the human physical capacity to dig a hole barehanded. Or consider a calculator: it surpasses a human's cognitive capability to perform arithmetic operations many times. Similarly, AI in its multiple forms and existing systems is yet another tool, albeit a highly sophisticated example.[8]

Aristotle on *Scholē* and Self-Moving Tools

Aristotle's disdain for arduous labour is well known. For him, *douleia* – hard, slavish labour – was the activity of slaves (*douloi*), even if he did not consider all labour to be equally slavish. There are qualitative distinctions between *technites* (craftsmen, artisans), *chernites* (manual labourers) and, of course, *physikoi douloi* (natural slaves) throughout *Politics*, yet all were excluded (along with women) from Aristotle's conceptualization of the good *polis*.[9] One of the main reasons for this exclusion was their lack of free time and their inability to engage in the virtuous activity of political rule and, more importantly, *scholē*. The latter is leisure time spent in self-cultivation by engaging in philosophical contemplation.[10] Aristotle's view of the relationship between work and *scholē* is best exemplified in his claim that 'it is thought that human flourishing (*eudaimonia*) is in *scholē*: we work (*ascholoumetha*) so that we may engage in *scholē*, and make war that we may live in peace' (Aristotelis 1894: 1177b4-6). Although the word *ascholoumetha* here literally means 'busying', it makes sense to translate it as 'work'. In any case, the Aristotelian principle is thus that human flourishing requires us to work for the sake of free time in order to freely cultivate our rational (and, we may add, creative) powers. If, then, anyone spends all of their time during the day working to produce the necessities of life and has no time for self-cultivation, then their life is slavish – they are governed by the alien force of necessity only, and therefore should be excluded from the *polis* of 'our prayers'.

This exclusion is detestable and has been rightly criticized many times, yet there is a materialist twist in Aristotle's argument. In the famous passage which, following Marx's readers of *Grundrisse*, we can call 'Aristotle's fragment on machine', Aristotle, as if contradicting his own notorious theory of natural slaves, claims that if we had tools which moved 'of their own motion' (*automatous*) and did their 'own work at the word of command or by intelligent anticipation', then master builders (*architektōn*) would not need subordinates and despots would not need slaves (Aristotle 1995: 1253b33-39). Whilst Aristotle had to imagine this situation (and the brilliance of his insight should not be underestimated), we do not. The AI built into the multiplicity of our automated tools today does what Aristotle could only imagine. There are cleaning robots, lawn-mowing robots, automated cars and trains, drones, industrial robots used in assembling, painting and welding, various service robots used in healthcare (including surgery) and hospitality, delivery robots in warehouses, customer service robots in stores, and agribots used in agriculture, to name but a few. All of these tools liberate us from different arduous, monotonous tasks or otherwise help us both in the process of production and in the daily life of social reproduction. However, the real import of Aristotle's insight is the claim on the nature of social relations when in possession of such self-moving tools: the material necessity for despotic, alienated social relations will disappear when slaves (and slavish labour) in a variety of forms (including workers engaged in alienated wage-labour) are no longer needed.

Life as Activity

The relationship between work/labour and human flourishing should be seen in dialectical terms.[11] On the one hand, Aristotle's view of work (*ascholoumetha*) as busying ourselves in doing what is necessary[12] has a negative connotation in the sense that it takes time from the truly virtuous activity (*kat' aretēn energeia*) of actualizing our rational powers. On the other hand, flourishing human life for Aristotle is an activity that consists in the full actualization of our specific *ergon* (function or work) – *logos* (language and reason, whereby the development of rationality is inseparable from our ability to use language).[13] I have argued elsewhere that Aristotle's conception of *eudaimonia* should be expanded and framed in inclusive terms: human flourishing consists of all meaningful human activities which require the cultivation of our rational, creative, imaginative and other intellectual powers in pursuit of cultural and moral excellence (Bielskis 2017: 119–22). In other words, a good human life consists of meaningful activities, of practices that require us to exercise our specifically human – intellectual and moral – powers. Alasdair MacIntyre's conception of practices[14] and their place in a flourishing life, as a powerful re-articulation of Aristotle's thesis that the good life is the life of activity, is important in our attempts to understand the place of work in contemporary lives increasingly dominated by AI-driven self-moving tools. That is, if a flourishing life requires both the exercise of virtues and engagement in meaningful work as sustained effort through time in the pursuit of genuine human ends, then not all activities and work should be automated by AI and self-moving tools. Rather, only alienated labour should be automated. This claim – i.e. given that a flourishing life is a life of activity when engaging in meaningful, non-alienated work due to which our intellectual, moral and imaginative powers are systematically exercised, human relationships with tools should be based on the principle that self-moving tools should not take away from humans the work that is essential for our flourishing – is the normative premise and the main thesis of this chapter. In other words, only alienated labour should be automated, while meaningful activities and the work or labour[15] necessary for these activities should not. It is, therefore, important to spell out briefly what meaningful, non-alienated work/labour is. Doing so, together with the notion of flourishing lives as active rather than passive, will give us a normative yardstick by which to measure what human–machine relationships ought to be in order to enable flourishing, and will allow us to judge the actual human–machine relationships within the existing regime of digital capitalism.

Post-Work Thesis *vs* Non-Alienated Labour

The distinction between alienated and non-alienated labour is important, not least because there is a growing anti-work and post-work theoretical tradition.[16] This body of literature raises fundamental and important questions on the nature of work in capitalism against a background of rapid technological development and ongoing automation in the era of digital capitalism. Simplifying its main arguments, we can put its main thesis in the following way. Given the constellation of the forces of production *and* the relations of production in the current form of capitalism dominated by digital code (and/or information), unemployment caused by technological development and automation is both inevitable and desirable. The neoliberal form of capitalism is, therefore, contradictory: on the one hand, it continuously relies on the post-Protestant work ethic of self-reliance realized through paid employment and the ideology of hard work. On the other hand, its mode of production increasingly relies on digital code and information which, in their nature, are resistant to commodification and marketization (Mason 2015), while capital owners' investment in AI-governed self-moving tools is driven by their determination to save costs on variable capital in the form of wages. The normative part of the post-work thesis – that we should accelerate the development of the forces of production by politically demanding a life without work – also has the ethical aspect of the desirability of human life beyond work.

The essential claim of this chapter (and largely of the whole book) is that while this thesis is politically laudable and correct (both in terms of political demands to work less and in terms of the critique of the neoliberal system of wage-labour), dominant post-work theorizing is ethically dubious and, more importantly, presupposes bad metaphysics.[17] That is, politically, post-work theorists (e.g.

Srnicek and Williams 2015) are right. Indeed, given AI-driven automation, we should work fewer hours per day, and this should be one of the key programmatic requirements of progressive politics. However, its normative aspect is wrong, given our Aristotelian metaphysical premise that a flourishing life is a life of activity aimed at the exercise of moral, intellectual and aesthetic excellences and their objectification in a multiplicity of cultural forms. If we accept this metaphysical premise – and this book argues that we should – then any meaningful activity in pursuit of excellence requires sustained effort and, therefore, at least some work and/or labour. Without work, the objectivized cultural forms of excellence are not possible. The post-work thesis therefore potentially presupposes (even if its defenders would not acknowledge it) a society in which the quest for excellence is not valued. Such a society would be content with triviality or mediocracy at best, whereby all of the activities of its members are equally valued and where individuals respect and recognize each other for their mediocre attempts to live their 'human, all too human' lives of passive consumption.

If work as sustained effort through time in the pursuit of excellence is important, then so is the distinction between non-alienated meaningful labour and alienated labour. How, then, shall we conceptualize non-alienated labour?[18] The worst form of alienation is, of course, slavery, whereby the principle of movement lies outside the moving subject. Aristotle's definition of a slave (*doulos*) is appropriate here: a slave is a living tool (*organon*) who is not their own, but belongs to another person as their property (Aristotle 1995: 1254b20-24). The absolute character of alienation in slavery lies both in the fact of ownership – one belongs to another rather than to themselves – and because a slave is nothing else but an instrument of another. Alienation in slavery is thus presupposed by its despotic character, whereby *despotes* meant not merely 'master' but also a despotic – vertical and entirely one-sided – social relationship entirely for the sake of the owner and not for the sake of the actor. A slave is a piece of an instrument, as any other piece of property is. Our relationship with tools is in this sense despotic: a tool is for our benefit only; we exploit tools and property for the sake of our pleasure. Thus, the relationship between humans and their tools is exploitative and despotic in its very nature: tools as pieces of property are for the sake of our benefit only, and never for the sake of the tool itself. To treat a tool – a manmade object – as if it was an independent entity, to serve the tool or worship it, is to fetishize and deify it as if it was a golden calf.

Marx conceptualized wage-labour, referring to it as wage-slavery, partly in line with Aristotle's notion of slavery. Alienation involved in wage-labour lies in the fact that the source of the activity of the worker is external to them in several respects.[19] First, the activity of the worker is commanded and controlled by the alien force in as much as the process of production is organized by the external agency in the service of the owner of the means of production in order to maximize their surplus value. Second, the aim of the activity of the worker is also alien to the worker, as the end-product of their labour does not belong to them. Third, given the debilitating and fragmented nature of work (consider, for example, labour in a pin factory or micro-work today), wage-labour of this sort is forced (or involuntary) because its efficient cause is external to the agency of the worker. The necessity of one's physical survival is the force behind it; thus, people would not do the work if they had an independent means of subsistence.

Marx's witty description of wage-labour in capitalism as 'wage-slavery' is accurate in as much as the despotism in the workplace of a capitalist corporation removes any agency from the worker. The only difference is that the wageworker is free to choose where to work. Otherwise, the worker does not belong to themselves during the hours of work and, given the above conditions, is a mere tool for the creation of surplus value for the capitalist despot. Following the above description of alienated labour, non-alienated labour is therefore based on the structural recognition of the moral and intellectual agency of the worker. For labour (or work) in the pursuit of excellence to be non-alienated, it should meet at least some of the characteristics of a MacIntyrean practice.[20] Thus, we have defined non-alienated meaningful labour in the following way:

> any exertion of sustained effort through time in pursuit of practice-based activities – such as arts, sciences, or sports, but also family life and the necessary work of social reproduction (e.g. looking after or educating children, cooking, running the household, caring for the sick and ill; or productive activities such as architecture and construction, sustainable agriculture, journalism, etc.) – which are democratically governed by workers themselves and/or are self-governing when governance comes from inside the activity itself.
>
> (Bielskis 2024)

The notion of meaningful activities also includes those that contribute to genuine (common) goods (what, paraphrasing Aristotle, we can call *kalon* ends) – fighting poverty, the climate crisis, political and economic injustice, tyranny, diseases, etc. – and whose organizational forms are devoid of despotic verticality.

Notes on the Political Economy of the AI Industry

If sheep 'ate' humans in the sixteenth century and ended feudalism, will the self-moving tools of the twenty-first century swallow wageworkers and end capitalism? Of course, this question cannot be answered in this chapter, but we should keep it in mind. Once again, from the point of view of historical materialism, AI and self-moving tools should free us from alienated labour – from jobs that are monotonous and debilitating, from tasks that debase our creative powers, etc. – and enable us to pursue the *scholē* type of activities of self-cultivation. However, although there are a great number of self-moving tools which have made our daily tasks of social reproduction easier (think of domestic appliances which help us to clean, wash, mow, etc.), the fundamental patterns in working conditions and the length of the working day have not changed since the mid-1940s (Srnicek and Williams 2015: 118). Furthermore, given that workers in the AI industry are engaged in immaterial labour *par excellence*, as the influential arguments of *post-operaismo* suggest (Hardt and Negri 2000, 2004), the hope for the greater autonomy of labour from capital is, alas, far too optimistic (Steinhoff 2021). Thus, it is important to briefly look at the structural elements of the dominant political economy of digital capitalism, especially of the AI Industry. In doing so, we will also be in a position to sketch out some forms of (immaterial) labour in today's capitalism.

Defining AI

However, we first return to the question of AI as a tool. Although there are several competing definitions of AI, it is generally agreed that AI is a branch of computer science (Zerilli et al. 2021). Definitions vary from AI pioneer John McCarthy's conception of the ability to make 'a machine behave in ways that would be called intelligent if a human were so behaving' (McCarthy et al. 1955) to less human-centred definitions of AI as 'making machines intelligent', where 'intelligence is that quality that enables an entity to function appropriately and with foresight in its environment' (Nilsson 2010: xiii). What is essential, however, is that AI should not be confused with robots: AI is software, while robots are constructed mechanical bodies (Steinhoff 2021: 9). Self-moving tools run by AI systems are mechanically constructed artefacts, which are capable of orientation in their immediate environments and can learn autonomously. The principle of recursion is essential to AI-governed tools. That is, recursion in AI is a machine's ability to apply information which was produced as an output back into its own algorithm and process it as an input (Ibid.: 14). In other words, it is expanded repetition that is able to produce something new which 'cannot be executed in advance' (cf. Ibid.). Thus, a convincing definition of AI is 'the array of computational techniques intended to model some aspect(s) of intelligence (loosely defined) which are capable of overcoming barriers of finite time, data and resources and possibly capable of transferring learning from one domain to other' (Ibid.: 11). Existing AI systems, therefore, are computational techniques and, as Steinhoff rightly concludes, *AI does not think*. Thus, any speculations on all-powerful artificial general intelligence (AGI) are nothing but speculations, and will not be considered here.[21] Such a conceptualization of AI reinforces our preliminary conclusion that AI as such does not exist (not in the sense that AI as a field of computer science does not exist), but in the sense that its reality lies in its applications within the existing forms of AI, which all function as domain-specific tools. The intelligence of existing AI systems is domain-specific, and thus they surpass human intelligence in their specific computational domains in a similar manner to the way in which the use of a spade surpasses a human's ability to dig holes barehanded.

The Concentration of Power and the Subsumption of Labour by Capital in the AI Industry

AI research has undergone several historical changes, which also reflect general trends in its political economy. AI research began in the late 1950s with GOFAI (Good Old Fashioned Artificial Intelligence), which was funded primarily by public money, geared towards the military industry, and aimed at mimicking high-level cognitive human functions (one of the achievements of this kind of AI was the victory of IBM's Deep Blue over Gary Kasparov in a game of chess in 1997). AI research then moved through two 'winters' in the 1960s and 1990s before arriving at the artificial neural network approach of today, which enables machine learning (ML) and is made possible by the vast amount of data freely available on the internet. Digital capitalism, a term invented by Dan Schiller (1999), was made viable through the invention of the World Wide Web. The rise of giant capitalist platforms such as Google, Facebook/Meta and Amazon created a privatized infrastructure that enables research in ML and its commodification, which has accelerated since 2010. As Pedro Domingos fancifully yet not entirely inaccurately put it, ML, which relies on vast amounts of data, is 'the inverse of programming': 'computers write their own programs so we don't have to' (cf. Steinhoff 2021: 121). The giant digital platforms which provide ML technology with primary data now form a vicious circle. Platforms capture data through surveillance while ML relies on data for recursive training, and so the AI industry and surveillance go hand in hand (Ibid.: 134). Hence, Schiller's digital capitalism has been renamed surveillance capitalism (Zuboff 2019).

The key structural aspects of the political economy of the AI industry, therefore, can be defined as follows. Given the commodification and marketization of AI, there is strong competition between a dozen giant digital corporations and their respective countries (the USA, China, and more recently the EU), which, as Evgeny Morozov argues, invest billions of dollars into research and development in order to produce the same types of skills. These corporations create algorithms, collect data and feed this data into the newly created algorithms to produce new automated functions and tools. Market competition, therefore, is wasteful, as the same digital functions are repeatedly created; instead, they should be produced once through a socialized feedback infrastructure (Morozov 2019, 2020). The concentration of vast financial power within the ten or eleven largest AI-producing companies is also a significant factor: the largest investors in AI are digital platforms such as Google and Meta, which acquire data through surveillance.

James Steinhoff (2021), applying Harry Braverman's labour process theory, convincingly demonstrated that the hopes of *post-operaismo* theorists (Hardt and Negri 2000, 2004) – who argued that immaterial labour dramatically changes contemporary capitalism and that, since production is increasingly based on digital code and/or information, as non-rival and non-commodifiable, revolutionary cracks are visible in today's capitalism – are premature. Rather than seeing the greater autonomy of workers engaged in the AI industry, we see the opposite tendency: their greater control and labour's subsumption to the needs of capital. ML scientists, data engineers (the labour 'aristocracy' of the AI industry), data analysts, service workers and ghost workers – the very bottom of the AI labour barrel – all experience a high level of managerial control in different ways. ML scientists and data engineers are controlled through managerial methodologies and software tools (e.g. Agile and Scrum) which are very similar in their nature (but not in their form) to the Taylorist methods of managerial control. Thus, what Steinhoff's analysis shows is that labour is not autonomous from capital, but rather the opposite: in the AI industry, the enormous concentration of capital in the hands of large corporations makes labour a cog in the process of the valorization of capital. As Steinhoff put it, 'labour continues to be subjected to the valorisation of capital amid the proliferation of AI' (Ibid.: 215).

Conclusion

The main contention of this chapter has been that, given that existing AI systems function as tools, the further production and application of AI should be judged democratically and in view of the model of human flourishing sketched out above. What should and should not be automated ought to be decided, first of all, via the rational deliberation of a political community which values its members' human flourishing and sees its existence in terms of a life of activity in pursuit of moral and cultural excellence. This, as we have seen, is not how the AI industry nor the general political economy of digital capitalism work. Driven by wasteful market competition, AI and automation are advanced for the benefit of capital's interest – first and foremost, the interests of several giant platforms in pursuit of greater control, market shares and future profits. Existing ML technology, which relies heavily on huge amounts of data, fosters the capture of our personal information through our use of an increasing number of smart tools and appliances (phones, watches, TV sets, computers, etc.), which is then fed back into algorithms to sell us more commodities that we do not need.

The grim political economy of the AI industry adds yet another contradiction to the list within the neoliberal form of capitalism. The open-access policies of digital platforms such as Google and Meta provide services to their users free of charge in return for their personal data. The neoclassical economic dogma of 'perfect market competition determines the prices of private goods' collapses in the context of digital platform capitalism. Hence, a growing number of voices are beginning to conceptualize this contemporary form of capitalism in terms of Mariana Mazzucato's 'algorithmic rents' or Yanis Varoufakis's 'techno-feudalism'. If the power of these corporations is not seriously challenged, then the growth of the vicious loop between the development of AI and personal data capture will continue through marketized encouragement to buy more 'smart' appliances which already saturate our daily lives. 'Dumb', old-fashioned watches, toasters, washing machines, toys, etc., will soon not seem so dumb.

The political demands of post-work theorists are indeed correct: we do need more free time as a material condition for human flourishing and non-alienated meaningful labour in pursuit of moral and cultural embodiments of excellence. Thus, progressive social movements, trade unions and the parties of the left should demand a much shorter working day, universal basic income, and comprehensively de-commodified, democratically governed social welfare institutions. The possession of free time, given the sophistication of our forces of production, is one of the conditions (but not a guarantee!) for collective human flourishing. The normative condition of our flourishing is our ability to educate ourselves and new generations to value a life of moral, aesthetic and intellectual excellence in which meaningful activities, practices and their internal standards of excellence are collectively celebrated while individual achievements are universally recognized.

This brings us to the use of AI and current and future forms of automation. If our techno-utopian future is a future of self-moving tools meeting all our needs, what will happen to human powers, to our essential powers of imagination, deliberation, cognition, judgement and intellectual insight? Herein lies the real threat of AI.

The argument that AI – in the form of AGI or any of its other forms – can achieve high levels of intelligence and autonomy that surpass human capabilities and intelligence in all human spheres is a silly exaggeration at best. The superintelligence of AI is not the real threat – in fact, current forms of AI are rather primitive compared to the originality and insight of Shakespeare, Marx or Wittgenstein. Talk of supposed superintelligence and the singularity of AI is simply the fetishization of AI. As I have argued in this chapter, AI is a tool, should remain so, and ought not to be made into a fetish. Thus, the greatest danger lies in its deification, leading to more of our powers and decisions being given to AI.

The biggest threat lies in thinking that AI is omnipotent; that it can advise us on how to solve one or another ethical or political problem that only humans can solve. The threat here lies in the underestimation of human intelligence and creativity: when, due to a lack of confidence in our abilities, laziness, a desire for convenience, or complacency, we might hand over rational decision-making to AI. To do this would be to impoverish ourselves as humans, allowing calculating machines, tools of our own making, to colonize our culture and ourselves. It is this aspect of AI, rather than its supposed omnipotence, that is and will remain the biggest threat that it poses in the future.

Notes

1 For an outstanding analysis of the political economy of the AI industry and platform capitalism in general, see Phil Jones (2021: 66–7).
2 Inverted commas here mean that there is not and cannot be strict causal determination in the sense that Marx (being influenced by the naive scientism of the nineteenth century) occasionally used this term when talking about 'the laws of history'. A better word is 'influence', yet the order and direction of causality should be kept intact: indeed, the forces of production create the material conditions for the gradual establishment of a specific regime of property relations.
3 As Marx and Engels put it when replying ironically to the Left-Hegelians: 'it is possible to achieve real liberation only in the real world and by real means, that slavery cannot be abolished without the steam-engine and the mule jenny, serfdom cannot be abolished without improved agriculture, and that, in general, people cannot be liberated as long as they are unable

to obtain food and drink, housing and clothing in adequate quality and quantity' (Marx and Engels 1988: 44).
4 I have argued elsewhere that there is not and cannot be a strict determination in the form of one-directional causality between the material conditions (cause) and the self-images of the age (effect) in Marx's account of materialism. Such a reading is a vulgar misunderstanding of Marx. Thus, there can be many ideological images of our age which stem from the material conditions in which we find ourselves (Bielskis 2022: 224–8).
5 This process is described in detail in Chapter 14 of *Capital* (vol. 1).
6 Marx's historical analysis of the enclosure process in Chapter 27 of *Capital* (vol. 1) is worth rereading again. As he puts it, the 'Parliamentary form of the robbery is that of "Bills for Inclosures of Commons", in other words decrees by which the landowners grant themselves the people's land as private property, decrees of expropriation of the people' (Marx 1990: 885).
7 This section is a modified version of my editorial entry 'Apie robotus ir avis' [Of Robots and Sheep] of the first issue of the culture and politics journal *Lūžis* (Bielskis 2020a: 2–8). The thesis spelled out above is, of course, well-charted and travelled territory.
8 There is, of course, ongoing debate on whether AI is just another tool or whether it is something more than a tool. The thesis I want to defend in this paper is that it is. What complicates this claim is the complexity and variety of AI systems. The difference between AI and other tools is not only that AI systems extend human intelligence and surpass certain cognitive capabilities (after all, computers extend and surpass the human cognitive faculty of computation), but that AI's application takes numerous forms in the different domains of human life. There is no AI as such, but different systems of AI which function as tools.
9 For a critique of Aristotle's conceptions of the household (*oikos*) and *oikonomia*, including his conception of natural slaves, see Bielskis (2017: 90–5, 2020b).
10 For an excellent account on the importance of *scholē* for *eudaimonious* life, see Kostas Kalimtzis (2017).
11 I have argued that although labour, work, activity and practice are not synonymous concepts, there are good reasons not to compartmentalize them and to treat them as interchangeable (see Bielskis 2024).
12 When discussing the blessedness of contemplation, Aristotle argues that the political life of moral virtues also involves *ascholoumetha*. Politics, even if it is a virtuous activity (*praxis*) essential to human flourishing, is less *eudaimonious* than the life of *scholē* as the actualization (*energeia*) of our contemplative and intellectual powers (see Aristotelis 1894: 1177). Thus, the politics of the best constitution, the *polis* of 'our prayers', will be directed to

the life of *scholē* as free time used in intellectual self-cultivation. However, the true sphere of necessity is *oikos* and *oikonomia* – the household and its management – where the most essential yet ephemeral (*ephemeron*) human needs are met.

13 Aristotle's formulation of *eudaimonia* in *Politics* is as follows: '*eudaimonia* is the best (*ariston*) and it consists in the actualisation (*energeia*) and perfect use/employment (*chresis*) of excellence (*aretē*)' ("ἐστὶν εὐδαιμονία τὸ ἄριστον, αὕτη δὲ ἀρετῆς ἐνέργεια καὶ χρῆσίς τις τέλειος") (Aristotelis 1957: 1328a36–7). A similar claim within the framework of his so-called function argument is repeated in the *Nicomachean Ethics*: *eudaimonia* is 'activity of the soul in accordance with […] the best and most complete excellence (*aretē*)' (Aristotelis 1894: 1098a16–17).

14 MacIntyre defines practice as 'any coherent and complex form of socially established cooperative human activity through which goods internal to that form of activity are realized in the course of trying to achieve those standards of excellence which are appropriate to, and partially definitive of, that form of activity, with the result that human powers to achieve excellence, and human conceptions of the ends and goods involved, are systematically extended' (MacIntyre 1985: 187). Examples of practices are chess (and other sports), physics, mathematics, philosophy (and other sciences), portrait painting, the composition and performance of music (and other arts), farming and agriculture, fishing (and other similarly complex productive activities), family life and politics as collective deliberation in the pursuit of common goods. MacIntyre's notion of practice and his philosophy in general has also influenced theoretical debates on meaningful work (see, e.g. Beadle and Knight 2012, Beadle 2019, Moore 2017; Breen 2019). See also Chapters 2 and 4 of this volume.

15 On the importance of understanding 'labour', 'work', 'practice' and 'activity' as intersecting and complementary concepts, see Bielskis (2024).

16 One of the boldest arguments for both the anti-work and post-work theses are John Danaher's claims in his *Automation and Utopia*, where he states that 'work is bad and getting worse, and we should welcome its technological elimination' (Danaher 2019: 54). A more subtle analysis of the anti-work and post-work theses within the history of modern work ethics is Kathi Weeks' *The Problem with Work* (2011) and Peter Fleming's *The Mythology of Work* (2015). The latter argues for the refusal of work within the context of the critique of neoliberal political economy. Nick Srnicek and Alex Williams' *Inventing the Future* (2015) is perhaps the most politically developed argument for a post-capitalist modernity without wage-labour, made possible through technological advancements in automation, robotics and the comprehensive institutions of the welfare provision coupled with

universal basic income. One of the earliest arguments for the necessity of thinking about the future of technological unemployment is Jeremy Rifkin's *The End of Work* (1995). There are many other examples, of course.

17 See also Jeff Noonan's chapter in this book on 'Artificial Intelligence, Alienation and the Existential Conditions of Human Flourishing'.
18 For a full argument that spells the distinction between alienated labour (and the selected history of theorizing alienation) and non-alienated meaningful labour, see Bielskis (2024). What follows here is its short, revised summary.
19 See also Ruth Groff's chapter on 'A Note on Marx, Alienation and Technology'.
20 On the relationship between MacIntyrean practices, work and recognition see Matthew Sinnicks, Efuntomi Wosu, and Craig Reeves's chapter on '"Mild Preparations": Work, Practices and the Internal Good of Recognition'.
21 A good example of such speculation is Nick Bostrom's (2014) celebrated and attention-grabbing attempt to warn humanity against the future dangers of AI.

References

Aristotelis (1894), *Ethica Nicomachea*, ed. I. Bywater, Oxford: Oxford University Press.
Aristotelis (1957), *Politika*, ed. W. D. Ross, Oxford: Clarendon Press.
Aristotle (1995), *Politics*, ed. R. Stalley, trans. E. Barker, Oxford: Oxford University Press.
Beadle, R. and Knight, K. (2012), 'Virtue and Meaningful Work', *Business Ethics Quarterly*, 22 (2): 433–50.
Beadle, R. (2019), 'Work, Meaning and Virtue', in Ruth Yeoman et al. (eds), *The Oxford Handbook of Meaningful Work*, 73–87, Oxford: Oxford University Press.
Bielskis, A. (2017), *Existence, Meaning, Excellence*, London: Routledge.
Bielskis, A. (2020a), 'Apie robotus ir avis', *Lūžis*, 1: 2–8.
Bielskis, A. (2020b), '"Managers would not need subordinates and masters would not need slaves": Aristotle's *Oikos* and *Oikonomia* Reconsidered', in A. Bielskis, E. Leontsini and K. Knight (eds), *Virtue Ethics and Contemporary Aristotelianism*, 40–57, London: Bloomsbury.
Bielskis, A. (2022), 'Against the Self-Images of Our Age: Questioning the Philosophy of Difference', in S. Maletta et al. (eds), *Practical Rationality & Human Difference*, 223–36, London: Mimesis International.

Bielskis, A. (2024), 'Theorizing Meaningful Non-Alienated Labour', *Critique: Journal of Socialist Thought*, 52 (1): 41–57.
Bostrom, N. (2014), *Superintelligence: Paths, Dangers, Strategies*, Oxford: Oxford University Press.
Breen, K. (2019), 'Meaningful Work and Freedom: Self-Realisation, Autonomy, and Non-Domination in Work', in R. Yeoman et al. (eds), *The Oxford Handbook of Meaningful Work*, 51–72, Oxford: Oxford University Press.
Castoriadis, C. (2005), *The Imaginary Institution of Society*, Cambridge: Polity Press.
Danaher, J. (2019), *Automation and Utopia*, Cambridge, MA: Harvard University Press.
Fleming, P. (2015), *The Mythology of Work: How Capitalism Persists Despite Itself*, London: Pluto Press.
Hardt, M. and Negri, A. (2000), *Empire*, Cambridge, MA: Harvard University Press.
Hardt, M. and Negri, A. (2004), *Multitude: War and Democracy in the Age of Empire*, London: Penguin.
Jones, P. (2021), *Work without the Worker: Labour in the Age of Platform Capitalism*, London: Verso.
Kalimtzis, K. (2017), *An Inquiry into the Philosophical Concept of* Scholē: *Leisure as a Political End*, London: Bloomsbury.
MacIntyre, A. (1985), *After Virtue*, 2nd edn, London: Duckworth.
McCarthy, J., Minsky, M., Rochester, N. and Shannon, C. (1955), 'A Proposal for the Dartmouth Summer Research Project on Artificial Intelligence'. http://www-formal.stanford.edu/jmc/history/dartmouth/dartmouth.html (accessed 2 April 2024).
Marx, K. ([1859] 1904), *A Contribution to the Critique of Political Economy*, Chicago: Charles H. Kerr & Company.
Marx, K. and Engels, F. (1988), *The German Ideology*, New York: Prometheus Books.
Marx, K. (1990), *Capital*, vol. 1, London: Penguin.
Mason, P. (2015), *Postcapitalism: A Guide to Our Future*, London: Penguin.
Moore, G. (2017), *Virtue at Work: Ethics for Individuals, Managers, and Organisations*, Oxford: Oxford University Press.
Morozov, E. (2019), 'Digital Socialism? The Calculation Debate in the Age of Big Data', *New Left Review*, 116/117: 33–67.
Morozov, E. (2020), 'Digital Socialism'. https://www.eurozine.com/digital-socialism/
Nilsson, N. (2010), *The Quest for Artificial Intelligence*, Cambridge: Cambridge University Press.
Popper, K. R. (1961), *The Poverty of Historicism*, New York: Harper & Row.

Rifkin, J. (1995), *The End of Work: The Decline of the Global Labor Force and the Dawn of the Post-Market Era*, New York: Putnam Books.

Schiller, D. (1999), *Digital Capitalism: Networking the Global Market System*, Cambridge, MA: The MIT Press.

Smith, A. (2007), *An Inquiry into the Nature and Causes of the Wealth of Nations*, Petersfield: Harriman House.

Srnicek, N. and Williams, A. (2015), *Inventing the Future: Postcapitalism and a World without Work*, London: Verso.

Steinhoff, J. (2021), *Automation and Autonomy: Labour, Capital and Machines in the Artificial Intelligence Industry*, Cham: Palgrave Macmillan.

Thompson, E. P. (1991), *The Making of the English Working Class*, London: Penguin Books.

Weeks, K. (2011), *The Problem with Work: Feminism, Marxism, Antiwork Politics, and Postwork Imaginaries*, Durham, NC: Duke University Press.

Zerilli, J., Maclaurin, J., Gavaghan, C., Knott, A., Liddicoat, J. and Noorman, M. (2021), *A Citizen's Guide to Artificial Intelligence*, Cambridge, MA: The MIT Press.

Zuboff, S. (2019), *The Age of Surveillance Capitalism: The Fight for a Human Future at the New Frontier of Power*, New York: Public Affairs.

2

Technē *in the Conflicts of Modernity*

A MacIntyrean Approach to Technology

Kelvin Knight and Joe Simpson

Technē was opposed by ancient Greeks to *phronesis*. Both were intellectual excellences or virtues. Both were forms of reasoning and judgement about how to act, informed by others' teaching and one's own experience. However, whereas *phronesis* was the virtue prized by citizens – that is, by the virile warriors who would dirty their hands only with the blood of the enemies of their own, particular city-state (*polis*) – *technē* was the excellence befitting their most prized slaves. The *technai* were the sets of skills exercised in such crafts as the doctoring practised by Aristotle's father, Nicomachus. Whereas Nicomachus used his *technē* to produce health in his patient, a citizen cultivated his own character in free and communal exercise of his *phronesis*. Whilst such exercise constituted ethical practice (*praxis*), which (like the purely conceptual activity of *theoria*) is undertaken for its own sake and for the good of the actor (and, ideally, for the political community of citizens), *technē* is only exercised for the sake of its product or performance. This distinction was theorized by Aristotle in his *Nicomachean Ethics* (Aristotle 2019: 104–7).

This distinction has more recently been rethought by another doctor's son, Alasdair MacIntyre, overcoming Aristotle's own failure to think his way beyond the self-serving social prejudices of those who paid himself and his father. This MacIntyre did in *After Virtue: A Study in Moral Theory* (1981), the argument of which he composed in America during the 1970s, after abandoning Britain and its New Left. Only around the decade's end did he turn his historical focus from the moral philosophizing of Hume, Kant, Hegel and Nietzsche to characterize his argument as a reworking of Aristotle's ethics. In effect (as became evident in subsequent work), *After Virtue* dispensed with Aristotle's distinction between *phronesis* and *technē* as the intellectual excellences of those engaged in, respectively, *praxis* and *poiesis* or, that is, practice and production.

Back in Britain, MacIntyre had considered it 'politically revolutionary' to understand '"socialism as the extension and culmination of the freedom and enterprise already displayed by the worker"' (MacIntyre 1963: 35, quoting Eugene Kamenka). This he wrote at the time his friend and fellow Workers' Educational Association tutor E. P. Thompson published *The Making of the English Working Class*, directing academic attention in America, also, to workers' historical struggle against their alienation from management of their own labour. Craft skills, craft unionism and whatever rights workers had won over the conditions and exercise of their own labour were defended by the American Federation of

Labor, even at the expense of efforts to unionize unskilled workers in such massive industries as steel and automobiles where the likes of Henry Ford, applying the 'scientific management' theory of Frederick Winslow Taylor, deprived workers of all vestiges of craft control over their own productive actions. Such deskilled American workers cooperated with the 'New Deal' government of Franklin Delano Roosevelt – who recruited as adviser Adolf Berle, legal theorist of corporate ownership's division from managerial 'control' – to establish rights to collective bargaining with their corporate employers, exercised through new, non-craft, industrial unions. In 1974, a veteran of such struggles, Harry Braverman, theorized the social loss of workers' self-management in *Labor and Monopoly Capital: The Degradation of Work in the Twentieth Century*. Apprenticed as a coppersmith, he 'enjoyed ... working as a craftsman' and, even whilst welcoming 'science-based technological change', 'always resented' how workers were 'systematically robbed of a craft heritage' by the capitalist deskilling which denied them 'the craft satisfaction that arises from conscious and purposeful mastery of the labor process' (Braverman 1974: 6–7). He analysed that systematic denial in terms of a progressive social division of productive functions between managers' 'conception and execution' by workers (Braverman 1974: 50–1, 112–21, 124–6, 171, 316, 445–7), under which the latter perform actions minutely preordained by those Taylorist managers, after acknowledging Aristotle's analysis of productive 'labor' or 'art' in terms of initial 'conception' and consequent 'execution' as purposively '*intelligent action*' (Braverman 1974: 46). Management's etymological origin he identified in humans' 'hand[ling]' of horses (as tools, with or without harnesses), whilst analysing capitalists' desire for similarly 'total economic, spiritual, moral, and physical domination' of their human resources, 'to impose their will upon their workers', and to suppress 'tradition, sentiment, and pride in workmanship ...

as manifestations of a better [human] nature' (Braverman 1974: 67-8). Updating what the first volume of Marx's *Capital* said of 'the labour process' with, most notably, C. Wright Mills's account of 'the new universe of management and manipulation' (Mills 1951: xv and *passim*), Braverman made much of workers' managerial 'manipulation' (Braverman 1974: 15, 30, 145-6, 150-1, 417) and of Soviet Marxism's adoption of the mechanical and administrative 'technology of capitalism' (Braverman 1974: 12). In this spirit, his analysis of capitalist systematicity suffered his 'self-imposed limitation to the "objective" content of class and the omission of ... "subjective"' (Braverman 1974: 27) struggles, enjoyments and honest, justifiable resentments such as those that motivated its own conception and brilliant literary execution. Even his fellow American Marxist, the altogether less proletarian Paul Sweezy, was left looking forward to someone inquiring into more 'subjective aspects' (Sweezy 1974: x).

The idea of 'manipulation' is crucial to the argument of *After Virtue*'s first half, where MacIntyre criticizes the failure of 'the Enlightenment Project of Justifying Morality' (MacIntyre 1981: 35, 49) for warranting an 'emotivist culture' (MacIntyre 1981: 21, 59) incapable of distinguishing a veritable ethic from a manipulative will to power. Having long endorsed Marxist criticism of 'the fetishism of commodities', whilst also criticizing Marxism for failing to exceed an ethics of 'rights' or of 'utility', he now added, as a fourth 'moral fiction', the 'fetishism ... of bureaucratic skills' conventionally attributed to 'the manager, that dominant figure of the contemporary scene', who characteristically claims 'to possess systematic effectiveness in controlling certain aspects of social reality', especially 'the manipulation of human beings into compliant patterns of behavior' (MacIntyre 1981: 101, 71). Such a 'technologist of human behavior' regards his manipulative action as 'the imprinting of his own will on ... society' and, 'as Marx saw ... the expression of his own rational autonomy', in contrast to that which he considers as the predictable behaviour of those subject to his supposedly scientific management. Here, like Braverman, MacIntyre traced how 'intellectual prophecy became social performance' (MacIntyre 1981: 81; for elaboration, see MacIntyre 1998). Where he differed was in rejecting Marxism's supposedly social scientific distinction of a predictive and evaluatively neutral objectivity from a subjectivity with which may be identified both emotions and ethics. His rejection of this characteristically modern distinction is what finally prompted him to expressly abandon post-Enlightenment moral philosophy for a more Aristotelian conceptual scheme and, yet, to retain modernity's sociological and historiographical insights in rejecting, also, Aristotle's own elitism (MacIntyre 1981: 149–50).

It is in *After Virtue*'s second half that MacIntyre replaced Aristotle's distinction of *praxis* and *poiesis*, action and production, with a stipulative distinction of 'practices' from organizational 'institutions' that is at once sociological and teleological. Sociologically, and economically, his new distinction sublated that of labour and capital. Like Braverman, the force of production that concerns him is labour. Without ever denying Marx's theories of commodity fetishism and of surplus value, his stipulative definition of a practice greatly extends and redescribes, in 'Neo-Aristotelian' terms (cf. MacIntyre 2016: 93–101), what others had discussed in terms of the labour process and of social class. Going to the extreme of rejecting Aristotle's 'metaphysical biology' (MacIntyre 1981: 56, 139, 152, 183; cf. his fitting of sociological to more traditionally Aristotelian teleology in MacIntyre 1999), he socialized Aristotelian teleology in imputing 'internal goods' to such shared social practices as those of medicine, farming and raising a family. Whilst following Aristotle in attributing a common good to the household and to the local political community, he extended the idea of common goods to communities of productive practice. He here described, in contemporary Aristotelian terms, what Braverman had called the enjoyments and satisfactions of working as a craftsman and as inheritor of a shared craft heritage, participating in the conscious and purposeful mastery of a productive process of conception and execution. As MacIntyre himself famously put it, a practice is a

> coherent and complex form of socially established cooperative human activity through which goods internal to that form of activity are realized in the course of trying to achieve those standards of excellence which are appropriate to, and partially definitive of, that form of activity, with the result that human powers to achieve excellence, and human conceptions of the ends and goods involved, are systematically extended.
>
> (MacIntyre 1981: 175)

The goods involved he analyses into two kinds: 'first of all the excellence of the products, both the excellence in performance by the [producer] and that of each [product] itself', and, secondly, 'the good of a certain kind of life' (MacIntyre 1981: 177). The excellence of producers' reasoning and acting, and of their consequent products, are goods that Aristotle categorized apart from the ethical excellences of masterful, patriarchal citizens. Rejecting this distinction, MacIntyre's plurality of *technai*, of productive practices and practical rationalities, combines the goods of *praxis* with those of *technē*.

The discipline of personal, participative emulation of impersonal standards of performative and productive excellence schools practitioners in not only technical but also social, moral excellence. As MacIntyre emphasized in concluding *After Virtue* (and elaborated throughout a later book, MacIntyre 1990), 'to cut oneself off from shared activity in which one has initially to learn obediently as an apprentice learns, to isolate oneself from the communities which find their point and purpose in such activities, will be to debar oneself from finding any good outside of oneself' (MacIntyre 1981: 240). Such socialization teaches practitioners to desire goods greater than the satisfaction of their more immediate, subjective urges, as he illustrated with the eminently apolitical Wittgensteinian example of chess. Although an excellent chess player is able to defeat opposing players, this ability will not be cultivated by winning through cheating under the rules that are constitutive of the game. One improves oneself by acknowledging and emulating the intellectual virtues of others, and one cultivates one's moral virtues through such emulation and by disciplining oneself to acquire, exercise and improve one's own skills. Whilst one might hone one's skill by playing against a computer, self-discipline is a moral virtue internal to the human person. Eventually, one might become so good at chess that one can improve even grandmasters' understanding (including that of those who programme chess computers) of the game itself, as a shared practice with a common good.

Such an account of practices improved upon those previously given by Wittgenstein and Rawls through its expression in terms of goods and moral virtues as well as of intellectual skills. For Rawls, in contrast, 'nothing essential for the theory of the good depends upon' 'the Aristotelian Principle' by which one is motivated to prefer 'playing chess to playing checkers' (Rawls 1971: 426–7) or tic-tac-toe. For MacIntyre, in contrast, it is through participation in practices that one learns, with others, how to understand both one's own good and, more theoretically, *the* good. Accordingly, one crucial move by MacIntyre was to make *After Virtue*'s account of practices the foundation for its further accounts of one's self-understanding, in society with others, and of philosophical traditions, as shared understandings. One gains self-understanding through pursuit of particular goods, and through understanding the point and purpose of such goods from and in conversation with others, whilst tradition (and what MacIntyre soon came to differentiate as rival traditions; MacIntyre 1988 and 1990) is the sum of such historically acquired understandings. Together, the concepts of a practice, of narratable self-understanding and of tradition comprised his reformulated, contemporary Aristotelian 'core concept of the virtues' (MacIntyre 1981: 174–209).

His further crucial advance was to distinguish practices from institutions. Whereas Wittgenstein or Rawls had treated the two terms as synonyms, MacIntyre used *institutions* to denote organizations. Whereas practices are the schools of the virtues, the interpersonal currencies of 'money, power and status' are those that structure institutions and into which institutions' participants are characteristically enculturated. Although sociological, MacIntyre did not intend this distinction as some amoral social ontology. Rather, it is an argument about ethics. The primary point is that common goods internal to shared practices should be defended against corruption by managerial and bureaucratic manipulation and corruption. Whereas Rawls called justice the first virtue of institutions, on *After Virtue*'s account it is one of the virtues that practitioners characteristically exercise toward one another. Justice is also a virtue that practitioners need to exercise in resisting manipulation and corruption by those who characteristically subserve goods external to their own shared practice. To the commonplace that 'organization – bureaucracy – is inescapable in advanced industrial technology' (Galbraith 1974: 17), MacIntyre had already long responded that organizational structure embodies 'certain attitudes and beliefs in both managers and managed', so that 'how society is organized and how people are conscious of and respond to this organization' (MacIntyre 1962: 22) constitute what, in *After Virtue*, he called 'a single causal order' (MacIntyre 1981: 181).

Whilst liberals, utilitarians and Marxists are all apt to be dismissive of producers' traditional virtues, skills and knowledge, MacIntyre sees such attributes as the social grounding of intellectual progress.

After Virtue attacks only the 'moral fiction' of 'managerial expertise' (MacIntyre 1981: 70–86, 101–2) claimed by 'the technologist of human behavior' (for what Braverman had called 'organizational skill', back when he hoped that 'engineering skill' might again become more important 'than rationalization of labor', Braverman 1966: 20–1), *not* the real expertise claimable by technologists of, for example, computing (MacIntyre 1981: 81, 90). The ethical issues about technology are those of the end, or good, for the sake of which technology is to be employed, and of whether decisions about technological means are to be made by those who prioritize goods internal to the relevant practice or by managers concerned only with the money, power and status to be accumulated and distributed by the relevant institution. The ethical challenge is that modern technologies are normally used by managers to justify their own, greater remuneration, power and status within an institutional division of roles in which they make the decisions and workers make only the products. In such an institutionalized world, workers are apt to be alienated not only from the products of their labour but also from decisions about how to conduct their productive activity. Whereas premodern was *technē* considered an attribute of the producer themself, modern technology tends to be used to dominate and control workers so that they have no control over their own actions. Increasingly, workers are denied any responsibility other than that to their managers.

After Virtue's ultimate opponent is Friedrich Nietzsche, for whom one's manipulation of others is an expression of a motivational 'will to power'. *After Virtue* does not deny such a will; to the contrary, each of its two argumentative halves concludes with fulsome acknowledgement of the danger to which Nietzsche alerted modern moralists, even whilst denying it any ahistorical impersonality or objectivity. The book's own warning is that the will to power is now disguised by claims to 'bureaucratic authority' that are embodied within interpersonal hierarchies of 'successful power' (MacIntyre 1981: 25), warranted by what the book's first half argues are moral and sociological fictions of managerial effectiveness. Its account of Nietzsche's moral and historical significance is prefaced by the proposition that 'a metaphysical belief in managerial expertise has been institutionalized in our corporations' (MacIntyre 1981: 102). A Nietzschean might well now consider Elon Musk as our contemporary Achilles or, better, as our manipulative Odysseus. For MacIntyre, the likes of Henry Ford, Frederick Winslow Taylor and Elon Musk are historically particular, cultural phenomena, characteristic of our emotivist, 'expressivist' and, especially now, 'technologically mesmerized culture' (MacIntyre 2016: 67–8, 148). Everywhere, human action may appear to be being displaced by process (Runciman 2023); everywhere, an impersonal will to power may appear to be cultivated within, and by, institutional hierarchies. However, MacIntyre gives us philosophical reason to think that there are limits to the effectivity of such technological and cultural processes, because human beings should, can and do resist.

MacIntyre's basic ethical point in *After Virtue* is that the kinds of life occupied in productive vocations, in which participants devote themselves to intellectually cooperative pursuit of common goods and standards of performative excellence, are more conducive to, and paradigmatic of, lives of moral excellence than are lives spent in competitive pursuit of money, status, and power over others. After writing the book, he embraced a specifically Thomistic Aristotelianism and converted to Catholicism, considering it as modernity's principal institutional bearer of that theoretical tradition of moral enquiry. Capitalist corporations, like bureaucratic states, he regards as institutionalized errors, even whilst, like Braverman, welcoming the technological advances often associated with economic competition or military conflict, but which owe vastly more to intellectual, scientific enquiry, technical expertise and the honest, ethical pursuit of true excellence. In this, he considers his Aristotelian tradition to be a better theoretical expression of the ethos of practical, technical and inventive rationality involved in scientific and technological progress than those of either Enlightenment intellectualism or Nietzschean perspectivism. Whilst agreeing with Kant that humans ought not to be regarded only as means to one another's ends, he opposes both modern and postmodern, emotively expressivist ideologies for effectively legitimizing managers' overruling of producers' real expertise and shared practical rationality.

Although practical ethics may very well be thought 'irrelevant' to capitalism (MacIntyre 2015), which therefore requires legitimation through state regulation, Marx equated labour's division with its socialization, which under capitalism operates through exchange but which will, he predicted, be achieved under communism by some more collectively intentional means. For Marx, 'when the worker co-operates in a planned way with others, he strips off the fetters of his individuality, and develops the capabilities of his species [but] as a general rule, workers cannot co-operate ... unless they are employed simultaneously by the same capital, the same capitalist' (Marx 1976: 447). For Braverman, that capital was no longer a capitalist but a corporation, as 'the *internal* planning of such corporations becomes in effect *social* planning' (Braverman 1974: 268; Braverman's emphases). MacIntyre's approach is more sociological. For him, collective, cooperative intentionality does not require a single planner, whether individual or institutional. *Never* a proponent of 'Stalinist', 'state capitalist' central planning, he gave ample reason in *After Virtue* to anticipate the Soviet Union's imminent collapse. There are likely to be limits to which bureaucratic managers' exercise of their manipulative will to power can successfully demoralize us, and themselves, by deskilling everyone into automatons.

After Virtue's argument has been updated in MacIntyre's last book, *Ethics in the Conflicts of Modernity*; MacIntyre extends his ethical analysis of 'the distinctive hopes and fears of capitalist and technological modernity' (MacIntyre 2016: 121). Such analysis reveals 'two very different' kinds of institutional condition under which new technologies may be developed, as Indiana's early Cummins Engine Company (MacIntyre 2016: 171–2) or the early British Broadcasting Corporation (MacIntyre 2016: 130–1; Ongun 2015: 120–31) used:

> one a mode of practice in which workers are able to pursue ends that they themselves have identified as worthwhile, in the pursuit of which they hold themselves to standards of excellence that they have made their own, the other an organization of activity such that their work is directed toward ends that are the ends of administrators and managers imposed upon their activities. In the former the primary responsibility for the quality of the end products of the work lies with the workers, who in this respect are treated as agents with rational and aesthetic powers, even though their labor is still exploited. In the latter this primary responsibility is assumed by administrators and managers, and productive workers are treated as means to the ends of administration and management.
>
> (MacIntyre 2016: 131)

In the former condition workers are able, collectively, to exercise something like the *technē* of an individual Athenian slave using an ox or an oven, or of an individual Macedonian doctor administering medicine to a patient. Responsibility for the exercise of such technical expertise and judgement was, then, normally to a master or employer, just as it is now normally to administrators or managers, themselves accountable to yet higher bureaucratic hierarchs. The book does not pretend that it is possible to do any more than resist such domination. Indeed, soon after its completion its author was rewarded with dismissal from a British university by managerial diktat. It acknowledges that there is no foreseeable end to the institutionalized conflicts characteristic of capitalist modernity, claiming only that conditions are actualizable under which producers' resistance can succeed in allowing them some control over their own actions and exercise of their own judgement. In this, it reiterates the argument of *After Virtue*: theoretically, demoralization must be resisted by commitment to an Aristotelian understanding of practical reasoning capable of differentiating it from the 'modern', instrumental rationalities of state and capital; practically, it must be resisted by those sufficiently habituated into such a commonsensical understanding that they are committed to identifying, actualizing and defending veritably common goods.

The 'single causal order' constituted by practices and institutions is that which Marxists, above all, endeavour to explain as 'capitalism'. MacIntyre, in *After Virtue*, switched the theoretical focus *from* capital, or what he reconceptualized as institutions, *to* human labour, or what he re-theorized and pluralized as practices. He thereby avoided the epistemological crisis encountered by twentieth-century Marxists – including himself, previously – in trying to theorize the increasing dominance of American management and Soviet bureaucracy over not only labour but also capital. Using his understandings of both that dilemma and the history of ethics (and the history and philosophy of science; MacIntyre 1977), he represented an ancient scheme for conceptualizing human action, reworking it to, in part, take account of our contemporary, institutional constraints. Given those constraints, he proposed that 'the essential function of the virtues is clear. Without them, without justice, courage and truthfulness, practices could not resist the corrupting power of institutions' (MacIntyre 1981: 181).

We may return to Sweezy's lament about Braverman's attempt at a purely objective analysis of capitalist, managerial, Taylorist imperatives toward automation and workers' deskilling. It is to Braverman's credit that the way he introduced his analysis made so obvious his own motivation in undertaking it, and therefore made obvious his deliberate dissociation of his theoretical work from its non-theoretical inspiration in his productive practice as a member of that working class with the welfare of whom he was so profoundly concerned. In dissociating his aspiration to a predictive science from his own subjective understanding of workers' agency he was theorizing as a good Marxist; in rejecting such theoretical aspirations (cf. MacIntyre 2008: 271; Knight 2007: 104–10, 116–24, 131–2, 167–9), MacIntyre is able to appeal to workers' exercise of their subjective and collective agency independent of any 'democratic centralist' institution. In the cause of demoralizing work, the philosopher has understood himself, increasingly, as a contemporary Aristotelian. It was such dissociation, and the consequent eschewal of ethics, that caused him to abandon Marx for Aristotle in returning to first principles. It is our contention that, by taking MacIntyre's analytic road, much can be illustrated and explained in the practical, ethical history of technology. Before drawing more particular illustrations, the most general point must be made: the historical function of capital in dividing and demoralizing labour has been less generative of technological innovation than have been the collective roles and rationalities of producers' own, shared practices.

An Episodic History of Communication Technology

'Man is in his actions and practice, as well as in his fictions, essentially a story-telling animal' wrote MacIntyre in *After Virtue* (MacIntyre 1981: 201), and narrativity remains an important aspect of his ethics (e.g. MacIntyre 2016: 243–315). It is therefore perhaps appropriate to refer to communication technology to illustrate some of the historical and social scientific significance of the book's lexical ordering of how practices, narratives and traditions are mutually constitutive.

The interface between technology and communication was famously explored by Marshall McLuhan, who was, like MacIntyre, not only a Catholic but also a Thomist (Morrisey 2018). McLuhan coined the phrase 'the medium is the message' in the title of the first chapter of a book (McLuhan 1964) which sold over 1 million copies. So popular became the phrase that subsequent editions use it as the book's title. You might summarize his life with a different epitaph, 'the messenger is the message', for certainly McLuhan became more famous than read. But let us look at some key technology advances and appraise their impact.

Let us start with the Gutenberg press (Jarvis 2023). Its innovative use of movable typeface had profound and unanticipated consequences, most dramatically with regard to religion. Schism was not uncommon in Christianity; indeed, we may note that it was almost a norm. But every pre-Gutenberg schism ultimately ground to a halt. Let us consider the changes that the innovation facilitated. Prior to Gutenberg, books required scribes, which prevented their mass production and distribution. The ecclesiastical hierarchy was therefore able to monopolize the language and delivery of the Christian message. Although Luther's original ninety-five theses were handwritten in Latin, he quickly turned to German and to print. The Roman Catholic Church then lost control of the Christian message. Without the printed word, Luther would never have achieved critical mass before the inevitable counter-reformation. Guttenberg enabled both a pluralization of Christian churches and traditions and a sustainable rejection of clerical domination of religious practice.

Our second instance of consequential innovation comes from the late nineteenth century and moving pictures. (We owe this story to

David Puttnam, the film producer.) The Lumiere brothers were the first to present moving pictures to a paying audience. Unless you are an extreme film buff, watching these early pictures for more than a few seconds is hardly a pleasure. Actors come in and out of shot in a seemingly haphazard way. To modern eyes, it seems amateurish. But those early cinematographers were professional stills photographers. We all know that our first few attempts at photography often produce rather blurred pictures or ones that miss out key aspects. As skilled stills photographers, our first cinematographers ensured quality of framing and control of the camera to get the most important parts of the action. It took a younger generation, not brought up learning the craft of stills photography, to realize that moving pictures also meant you could move the camera, from which we get movies as we know them today. We thus see not merely a new practice (cinema) but a new set of practitioners (cinematographers).

Our third illustration concerns the invention of television, in which John Logie Baird was salient. Here we see how technological change affects the relationship between practitioners and the audiences who view the products of their practices. As with many inventions, television's success was facilitated by an additional technology. For a long time the number of British television channels was limited. Until the 1980s, Britain had only two and a half channels (the half being BBC2, which only started its limited evening transmission at 7.30 pm). For television schedulers, the key issue was how to attract a large audience. Shows like *Morecambe and Wise* could get audiences in excess of 20 million. Niche audiences were not a focus (unless required by the state broadcasting authorities). But with the advent of digital and satellite, we now have a plethora of channels. Unless, say, England reaches the final of an international soccer championship, the prospect of half the population watching the same thing at the same time seems far-fetched. As a consequence, schedulers now see the advantage of seeking out niche audiences. This switch from a broadcast to a narrowcast model also had further effects. Whereas in the 1970s the *Morecambe and Wise Christmas Special* would get a UK audience in excess of 25 million people, for Christmas 2023 the top rating programme was the King's Speech (literally, a recorded message by the King, not a repeat of the film), but its audience was 5.8 million, 20 million fewer than in the 1970s. The British Broadcasting Corporation still often uses the language of its first director-general, John Reith, in describing its social role as to inform, educate and entertain. For most of its history the institution's public priorities were in that order, even though entertainment was critical to the case for funding through the flat-rate, universal licence fee. But as audiences fragmented, the BBC benefited from Harvard academic Mark Moore's insight that if private organizations are driven by private profit, public organizations should be driven by the need to create public value (Moore 1997). Looking at how public value could be created, the BBC recalled another early motto: nation shall speak unto nation. One of the key characteristics of the BBC was that it always became the channel of choice for most British people at key moments such as a royal death, as evidenced by the viewing figures for the funerals of both Princess Diana and the late Queen, a royal marriage (Diana again) or a coronation. Indeed, the late Queen's own coronation prompted perhaps 1 million people to buy a television, and more than any other event prompted the presumption in the UK that every household would acquire a television. The 1966 Word Cup Final saw another uplift in sales. The institutional trouble with royal marriages, deaths or coronations, or cup finals, is that their occurrence is not under the corporation's control. So, BBC management started to consider how they could produce programmes that would provoke 'water cooler moments' (to use an American phrase) amongst a mass audience. So, we start to see the rise of management-induced formats, the most recent of which is that of *Strictly Come Dancing*, which, under various titles, has spread worldwide. In Britain, the word 'Strictly' is enough to denote the phenomenon, even to people who have never watched the programme.

This switch from broadcasting to narrow casting had a parallel effect on newspapers. In 1992, to the surprise of many, John Major won a fourth term in the UK general election. Famously, on the day of the election, the *Sun* newspaper's headline was 'If Kinnock wins today will the last person to leave Britain please turn out the lights'. The next day their headline was 'It's the Sun Wot Won It' – an exaggeration but with enough semblance of truth to have some credibility. But as newspaper circulation has plummeted, the truth now is that newspapers cultivate their readership by carrying stories their readers want. In other words, they are narrowcasting. Secondly, whilst newspapers may still help clarify agendas for their readerships, their readerships are less diverse in opinions than previously.

Our next illustration concerns Sony, for much of the second half of the twentieth century the most innovative of Japanese technology companies. Innovation has not always entailed commercial success, and commercial monopolies often ensure the success of inferior technologies. For example, Betamax was a superior technology to VHS cassettes but VHS achieved a significant market share first and Sony only dominated the professional market. A still more relevant example is the Sony Walkman, the forerunner of much of the way we now use our mobile phones. Before bringing it to market, many in the company thought there should be detailed market research to see if there was an appetite for such a device. They were overruled by the then president of Sony, who realized that people were not demanding something which they did not know was possible. To adapt the strapline of a famous American story, his approach was build it and they shall buy.

Our fifth illustration concerns typewriters. When first developed we had what were called manual typewriters, in reality a mechanical operation. The key challenge was to make sure that they keys did not get stuck together (the faster you typed, the more likely this was to happen). The solution was the QWERTY layout, which reduced the likelihood of this happening. Of course, with electronic typewriting this was not a problem but by then the QWERTY layout was ubiquitous, exemplifying 'path dependency'; the initial road taken by a new technology constrains its future routes.

The development of manual typewriters caused the appearance of typists. In sexist societies, this became an almost exclusively female role and, consequently, the older role of secretary was increasingly occupied by women. Indeed, secretarial work developed its own hierarchy, where 'promotion' was possible by working for a more senior person. The role continued even through the advent of the internet. The advent of mobile devices, most notably Blackberrys (a.k.a. 'Crackberrys') led to the 'discovery' that men could type; the role-switch having begun at the start of the internet rather than awaiting the advent of mobile devices able to access it (Graham 2023).

The late Clay Christensen (2016) observed how rarely the pioneers of one socially disruptive technology become the successful proponents of another – even when they are the inventors of that later technology. Christensen did not use MacIntyre's framing (he worked not in philosophy but first in management consulting and then in management education) but the parallels are clear – proponents of the old technology had their worldview framed by the traditions and practices of the older technology. (McLuhan made the parallel point that we see the future through the eyes of the past.) The roll call of companies who failed to understand the inventions they made is legion, perhaps the two most cited being Rank Zerox and Eastman Kodak.

Narrating technological change in terms of institutions, practices and traditions frees us from any presumption that technology is morally neutral. Jeff Bezos and a redundant shopfloor worker will view the increasing power of Amazon differently. Let us remember the insight of Yogi Berra, the great baseball player, that prediction is difficult. Both MacIntyre and Christensen remind us how difficult it is to understand the implications of radical innovation, even if we are the innovators.

'Intellectual property (IP) rights' illustrate what is at stake between the shared rationalities internal to productive practices and the will to power institutionalized in states and capitalist corporations. Legal protection of corporations' IP is justified as incentivizing innovation. Certainly, it incentivizes investment by the leisure class in corporations that expropriate the intellectual labour of practitioners they employ and manage, alienating those practitioners from the products of their own labour. Certainly, also, institutionalized incentives of money, power and status shape the resulting technologies. Here, we leave aside consequentialist concerns about the environmental impact of such shaping. Our concern here is with its social and moral impact. From a MacIntyrean standpoint, what is obvious is that 'when new technologies of production are deployed in dominant media institutions, the systemic constraints under which they operate in turn constrain the potential for improving the practice as such – technological potential is repressed because of the dominant orientation towards external goods' (Salter 2008: 40). IP is a crucial institutional instance, denying practitioners within institutions any power over their own innovations or those of their colleagues, denying practitioners the chance to freely use and experiment with those technologies, and granting the corporation's managers a veto over any effort by practitioners to develop the technology. If the legally monopolized technology will not make a considerable corporate profit, or if its use or development will not otherwise suit managers' interests, then it will not be used and cannot be further developed.

Against the character of the Nietzschean manager we may pit that of Tim Berners-Lee, inventor of the World Wide Web, whose will to knowledge evidently disguises no will to power. Needing no promise of IP to incentivize his innovation, he made it openly accessible and freely usable to everyone. Representing a new, practical 'community of [web] developers', he defeated every 'effort by any institution or company to "control" things' (Berners-Lee 1999: 79–80). His and their World Wide Web Consortium is no monopolistic corporation. The best way to ensure technically excellent, ethically educative and socially beneficial innovation is to trust the ingenuity of practitioners. Institutionally (as well as environmentally), a better world is possible.

References

Aristotle (2019), *Nicomachean Ethics*, 3rd edn, trans. Terence Irwin, London: Hackett.
Berners-Lee, T. (1999), *Weaving the Web: The Original Design and Ultimate Destiny of the World Wide Web by Its Inventor*, London: HarperCollins.
Braverman, H. (1966), *The Future of Russia*, New York: Grosset & Dunlap.
Braverman, H. (1974) *Labor and Monopoly Capital: The Degradation of Work in the Twentieth Century*, New York: Monthly Review Press.
Christensen, C. M. (2016), *The Clayton M. Christensen Reader*, Boston, MA: Harvard Business Review Press.
Galbraith, J. K. (1974), *The New Industrial State*, Harmondsworth: Penguin.
Graham, Y. M. (2023), *Jobs for the Girls*, London: Hachette.
Jarvis, J. (2023), *The Gutenberg Parenthesis: The Age of Print and its Lessons for the Age of the Internet*, London: Bloomsbury.
Knight, K. (2007), *Aristotelian Philosophy: Ethics and Politics from Aristotle to MacIntyre*, Cambridge: Polity Press.
MacIntyre, A. (1962), 'C. Wright Mills', *International Socialism*, 9: 21–3.
MacIntyre, A. (1963), 'Marx and Morals', *International Socialism*, 14: 35.
MacIntyre, A. (1977), 'Epistemological Crises, Dramatic Narrative and the Philosophy of Science', *The Monist*, 60 (40): 453–72.
MacIntyre, A. (1981), *After Virtue: A Study in Moral Theory*, Notre Dame, IN: University of Notre Dame Press.

MacIntyre, A. (1988), *Whose Justice? Which Rationality?*, Notre Dame, IN: University of Notre Dame Press.
MacIntyre, A. (1990), *Three Rival Versions of Moral Excellence: Encyclopedia, Genealogy, and Tradition*, Notre Dame, IN: University of Notre Dame Press.
MacIntyre, A. (1998), 'The Theses on Feuerbach: A Road Not Taken', in K. Knight (ed.), *The MacIntyre Reader*, 223–34, Cambridge: Polity Press.
MacIntyre, A. (1999), *Dependent Rational Animals: Why Human Beings Need the Virtues*, London: Duckworth.
MacIntyre, A. (2008), 'What More Needs to Be Said? A Beginning, although Only a Beginning, at Saying It', in K. Knight and P. Blackledge (eds), *Revolutionary Aristotelianism: Ethics, Resistance and Utopia*, 261–81, Stuttgart: Lucius & Lucius.
MacIntyre, A. (2015), 'The Irrelevance of Ethics', in A. Bielskis and K. Knight (eds), *Virtue and Economy: Essays on Morality and Markets*, 7–21, Farnham: Ashgate.
MacIntyre, A. (2016), *Ethics in the Conflicts of Modernity: An Essay on Desire, Practical Reasoning, and Narrative*, Cambridge: Cambridge University Press.
Marx, K. (1976), *Capital: A Critique of Political Economy*, vol. 1, trans. B. Fowkes, Harmondsworth: Penguin.
McLuhan, M. (1964), *Understanding Media: The Extensions of Man*, New York: McGraw Hill.
Mills, C. W. (1951), *White Collar: The American Middle Classes*, New York: Oxford University Press.
Moore, M. H. (1997), *Creating Public Value: Strategic Management in Government*, Cambridge, MA: Harvard University Press.
Morrissey, C. S. (2018), 'The Analogy of Marshall McLuhan', in R. Heynickx and S. Symons (eds), *So What's New About Scholasticism?: How Neo-Thomism Helped Shape the Twentieth Century*, 231–54, New York: De Gruyter.
Ongun, M. (2015), 'Reappraising Neoliberalism: Homo Economicus, Practitioners and Practices', in A. Bielskis and K. Knight (eds), *Virtue and Economy: Essays on Morality and Markets*, 109–33, Farnham: Ashgate.
Rawls, J. (1971), *A Theory of Justice*, Cambridge, MA: Harvard University Press.
Runciman, D. (2023), *The Handover: How We Gave Control of Our Lives to Corporations, States and AIs*, London: Profile Books, 2023.
Salter, L. (2008), 'The Goods of Community? The Potential of Journalism as a Social Practice', *Philosophy of Management*, 7 (1): 33–44.
Sweezy, P. M. (1974), 'Foreword', in H. Braverman, *Labor and Monopoly Capital: The Degradation of Work in the Twentieth Century*, New York: Monthly Review Press.
Thompson, E. P. (1991), *The Making of the English Working Class*, London: Penguin Books.

3

Algorithmic Management

The Corrupting Power of Technology

Pablo García Ruiz

Introduction

In recent times, digitization and the introduction of Artificial Intelligence systems have endowed technology with the ability, known as 'algorithmic management', to perform managerial tasks, such as coordinating workflows, selecting personnel, evaluating performance, and even imposing sanctions. In this chapter, we explore whether algorithmic management manifests the manipulative character that MacIntyre attributes to professional management. In the digital economy, it is the algorithm that holds the decision-making power and assigns workers the execution. This power is claimed on the basis of superior knowledge (algorithmic calculation) on how to achieve the greatest efficiency, a claim that does seem well founded. Algorithmic management is carried out, on the one hand, through surveillance and control of human workers and, on the other hand, through the discourse of persuasion typical of the freelance economy.

Algorithmic management improves workplace effectiveness but also introduces new threats to the balance between effectiveness and human excellence. Since work is a crucial element for human flourishing, it is vital to consider whether human labour can remain relevant in the search for a good life in our current technological scenario. This chapter addresses this question from a MacIntyrean perspective. First, it presents the MacIntyrean characterization of management. Then, it discusses the main features of the so-called algorithmic management. Finally, it discusses the manipulative character of this new kind of management and its impact on the possibility of human flourishing in the workplace.

MacIntyre's Critique of Management

In *After Virtue*, MacIntyre warns about management's amoral and manipulative nature (2007: 30–2). For MacIntyre, on the one hand, professional management tends to manipulate employees by treating them as mere means to the fulfilment of the manager's ends; and, on the other hand, managers are incapable of entering into a genuine moral argument since their role 'consists in matching means to given ends without assessing those ends' (Sinnicks 2018: 736). In modern organizations, managers 'restrict themselves to the realm of fact, the realm of means, the realm of measurable effectiveness' (MacIntyre 2007: 30). This inability to assess ends is not a matter of individual failing but of the social structure in which their role is displayed (Knight 2008: 43). Pleonexia is the driving force of modern productive work (Blackledge and Raptis 2020: 151). The harshness of competition and the immoderate drive for profit incite managers to prioritize achieving effectiveness objectives over pursuing any other kind of goods. The means–ends relationships are typically external to the goods that those who work seek, including the goods of their excellence as workers and as human beings.

Within capitalism, labour is made and valued as a commodity. As a result, work often becomes valued only as a means to production and consumption, and workers are correspondingly valued only for their producing and consuming functions (MacIntyre 2011: 315). The measure of human work is its cost-effectiveness (Ibid. p323). Professional managers leading all kinds of private and public bureaucratic organizations claim the authority to manage workers on the pretence that they have superior knowledge and experience on how to be effective. Such expertise and authority are assumed to be universally applicable and transferable from one organization to another, regardless of the activity carried out there (MacIntyre 2007: 26–7). Legitimated by this authority, organizations develop power structures to implement managerial decisions even against workers' opposition.

Despite this, MacIntyre (2007: 187–95) admits that institutions are necessary to sustain practices, formalize and enforce rules, and obtain and distribute resources. Practices are collaborative activities in which workers may learn and develop those skills required to excel as workers. Practitioners need to organize themselves to set standards, obtain resources and advance other common goals. To this end, universities, professional associations and business companies emerge. These organizations are a combination of practice and institution. While practices are concerned with internal goods (also called goods of excellence), institutions focus on the acquisition of external goods (or goods of effectiveness), such as money, power and prestige, which are necessary to sustain and nurture practices (MacIntyre 1988).

In practices, workers may also develop virtues, i.e. those qualities that enable agents to identify both 'what goods are at stake in any particular situation', and how one 'must act for the sake of the good and the best' (MacIntyre 2016: 392). The acquisition of goods of effectiveness is a necessary and valuable function of an organization as long as it is subordinate to the sustenance and development of the practices it hosts (Moore and Beadle 2006: 371–2). Therefore, management would be non-manipulative insofar as it defended the goods internal to work practices, the standards of excellence, and the common good of the organization's members (Moore 2017: 110–14). MacIntyre has called attention to some examples of non-manipulative management, such as the Deming-driven quality circles in Japanese companies (MacIntyre 2016: 245–8) that allow workers to exercise practical wisdom to deliver good products while developing their own professional and moral capacities.

However, the simultaneous pursuit of excellence and effectiveness typically causes tensions in organizations. There is a constant risk that the order of priorities will change and effectiveness considerations will prevail: 'The ideals and the creativity of the practice are always vulnerable to the acquisitiveness of the institution, in which the cooperative care for common goods of the practice is always vulnerable to the competitiveness of the institution' (MacIntyre 2007: 194). Good work is compromised when power structures deny workers control over their activity and, consequently, prevent them from cultivating their own goods, including those of personal excellence (Beadle and Knight 2012: 436–7). Moreover, current forms of work organization make it difficult for work activities to develop the characteristics of practices. For example, the vast factories with thousands of workers that produce gadgets and other objects on which our daily lives depend use highly standardized processes that do not require wisdom, creativity, or other professional skills (Mardosas 2020: 216). Much of this work can be and indeed is detrimental to human development, even debilitating and hazardous to health.

This MacIntyrean characterization of management as bureaucratic and value-free has been criticized as outdated since new and more substantive forms of management have arisen in the last decades (Knight 2017; Sinnicks 2018). In these years, there has been a proliferation of management discourses that explicitly include the question of the purpose of work and workers. For example, multiple leadership theories discuss human motivation and its different dimensions. However, many of these theories tend to support MacIntyre's central charge. Most of these new management theories use their knowledge of human motivation to generate new forms of manipulation of workers: 'While scientific management could justly be regarded as manipulative in that it saw workers as tools to be expertly controlled, the dominant forms of leadership are manipulative in that they attempt to use charisma and inspiration in place of rational persuasion' (Sinnicks 2018: 741). Similarly, the discourse of employees' participation in management, which promotes the involvement of workers in the company's decision-making, often ignores or uses, to the company's advantage, the ability of workers to deliberate on their own goals. In so doing, those management discourses thus become 'mechanisms of labour exploitation' (Blackledge 2023: 256).

The diffusion of information technologies in the workplace contributes to an increasing deskilling and individualization of work tasks (Vallor 2015: 108–10). MacIntyre's account of human flourishing and work lacks a comprehensive discussion of technology (Mardosas 2020: 216). However, this discussion is necessary, given its widespread use in all kinds of professions and jobs. Moreover, in the current technological scenario, the possibility of doing good work exceeds labour or legal considerations to become a moral issue.

MacIntyre's philosophy of work is based on the fundamental idea that 'there is a close connection between being a good human being and doing good work' (MacIntyre 2011: 323). Work is a means for us to flourish as human beings: 'It is in and through our engagement in such laborious and productive activities as farming, construction work, and the like, that a number of virtues much needed in our individual and communal lives are developed and exercised' (MacIntyre 2008: 275). It should be noted that, for MacIntyre, the work that helps to flourish is not an individual activity, which each person can carry out on his or her own. Human flourishing, i.e. the development of our physical, intellectual, moral and aesthetic powers, can only be realized 'in and through our social relationships' (MacIntyre 2011: 318). The achievement of one's own individual good requires the joint pursuit of goods common to the members of communities to which one belongs, be it the family, a neighbourhood association or the workplace. Individuals can attain their own individual goods only in and through the attainment of those common goods that they share with others. Thus, care for one's family, for one's friends, and for the ethos of one's workplace are characteristic elements of a good human life (MacIntyre 2016: 246). Therefore, 'doing one's work well rather than badly and recognizing the dependence of one's work on the work of a wide variety of others, and therefore how much one is in debt to those others, are as important in the moral life as telling the truth and keeping promises' (MacIntyre 2008: 275).

For MacIntyre, work has a substantive value in addition to its instrumental value. Work constitutes a central dimension of human flourishing when it becomes a part of the search for the good life. It stands then as a good for those who work and those with whom they collaborate to generate common goods.

However, when work is deprived of meanings that transcend mere utility, workers can no longer find in their work an activity that fulfils their personal and relational lives. It is precisely this effect that technology can produce when it takes control of work processes. Marx ([1932] 2009) asserted that certain technologies determine the social order, usually to reproduce the dominant-dominated dialectic. As a consequence, workers become alienated from the product of their labour (powerless over what happens to it), from productive activity (by losing connection with the labour process), from their species-being (the human creative capacity) and, finally, from other human beings because capitalism induces them to act as competitors, not as cooperators (Rodriguez-Lluesma et al. 2021: 158). From a different perspective, Heidegger also claimed against alienation since the essence of modern technology reduces both nature and human beings to a 'standing reserve' by ordering everything 'to stand by, to be immediately at hand, indeed to stand there just so it may be on call for a further ordering' (Heidegger 1993: 322). Both Heidegger and Marx, for very different reasons, of course, agree that technology alienates agents by objectifying them. Heidegger was a technophobe and gave birth to the tradition of the totalizing critique of technology as something that leads to an 'inauthentic life'. Marx, in essence, was a technophile because without technological advancement there cannot be any advancement in the forces of production, and without that, human progress (in the form of the communism of social humanity) is impossible. Heidegger criticized the essence of technology, while Marx criticized the consequences of technology in capitalism. MacIntyre adopts the Marxian idea that material, institutional and social conditions in which workers inhabit can alienate them from their practices and, therefore, from the possibility of their flourishing (Knight 2008: 44). Among such conditions, there is professional management, which is a producer of and is produced by alienated relations (Blackledge 2023: 252–4) proper to the capitalist social order.

Under these premises, the following section analyses the main features of algorithmic management as a technological structure increasingly present in current workplaces. Subsequently, the final section will explore whether it manifests the manipulative character MacIntyre attributes to professional management.

Algorithmic Management

With the advancement of technologies, the type of activities that machines can perform has been expanding from repetitive and simple tasks to complex and creative jobs such as designing objects, choosing transportation routes and predicting the success of specific commercial actions (Daugherty and Wilson 2018; Davenport and Miller 2022). The 'deep learning' that enables machines to perform these tasks relies on collecting and using large databases to develop and improve algorithms capable of computing optimal solutions for different purposes.

Algorithmic management relies on this large-scale collection and use of data to train learning algorithms that carry out coordination and control functions traditionally performed by human managers (Möhlmann et al. 2021: 1999–2001). Algorithms are now commonly used for human resource management activities (Parent-Rocheleau and Parker 2022: 2–3), such as recruiting and hiring new personnel (i.e. identifying candidates fitting given profiles), monitoring workers (i.e. collecting and reporting data on employees' behaviour during their work), performance management (i.e. algorithms displaying employees' performance rating or providing automated performance feedback), scheduling (i.e. algorithms setting employees' schedules or sending nudges for suggested working times), compensation (i.e. automated calculation of pay based on conditions and metrics), as well as applying positive or negative sanctions in the form of recommendation, warning, exclusion and job termination (i.e. automated termination decision-making or announcement).

Algorithm management has become especially widespread in the platform economy (Stark and Pais 2020: 53–5). Companies such as Uber, Airbnb, Udemy, TaskRabbit and TripAdvisor rely on algorithms for managerial tasks such as matching workers with customers, setting prices, handling logistics and conducting business communication. In this system of control, algorithms are programmed to make and implement decisions affecting labour, thereby limiting human involvement and oversight of the labour process (Parent-Rocheleau and Parker 2022: 4–6).

Algorithmic calculation is believed to lead to accurate outcomes in analysing and predicting complex relationships while eliminating unconscious human bias, with evidence indicating that such decisions outperform human management in the vast majority of cases in the everyday workload context (Kinowska and Sienkiewicz 2022: 23).

However, alongside this improvement in efficiency, there are other less positive consequences that not only occur at the same time but also become the conditions that make it possible. In particular, greater efficiency goes hand in hand with deficient communication and scarce transparency between workers and management.

The communication deficit between employees and management stems from the increasing automation of this communication. A paradigmatic case is those working for service platforms such as Uber, eBay and TaskRabbit. All communication between the platform's management and each of the workers (drivers, suppliers or furniture assemblers) takes place through the software designed for this purpose. If any worker has doubts, complaints or questions about the algorithm's decisions, he or she only receives preset answers through the app. There is no room for a genuine dialogue with any human manager. Moreover, if, by exception, the worker manages to reach a human operator, the latter will probably tell him that 'there is nothing she can do: it is a matter of the algorithm' (Curchod et al. 2020: 655).

It is the algorithm that has the power to match each potential customer with a specific worker. Thus, at Uber, it is the algorithm that selects a driver and offers him or her a ride at a specific price. Similarly, at eBay, it is the algorithm that selects and matches suppliers with consumers. At TaskRabbit, it is the algorithm that selects a few carpenters to access the job offers requested by users of the platform. It is always the algorithm that values, ranks, rewards or penalizes workers to the point of excluding them, even without notice, based on its calculations. Platforms are not required to provide reasons for these decisions to those who work for them. If they do provide them, the reasons offered are invariably cryptic, and the criteria for their decisions are unclear (Cutolo et al. 2021: 3).

Algorithms evaluate (rate) workers and classify them in rankings, according to which they offer job opportunities. Often, the criteria for calculating ratings are neither stable nor entirely comprehensible. This lack of clear criteria is why algorithms are often referred to as 'black boxes'. For example, on many platforms, it is neither clear what the minimum score is for not being excluded, nor to what extent the worker's acceptance and rejection ratios influence their position in the ranking, nor what parameters are used to recognize a worker as particularly valuable (Roberts and Zietsma 2018: 208). This communication deficit, although especially visible in the platform economy, is not limited to platform companies. Since the post-pandemic shift to remote working practices, any company has a range of tools, from tracking applications to productivity measurement software, to collect information about its workers and manage their behaviour.

This lack of communication and transparency shows that algorithmic management is not an automation of bureaucracy despite some superficial similarities between the two management styles (Noponen et al. 2023: 5). Algorithmic management is not a kind of digital Taylorism; it is a new, distinctive model (Stark and Pais 2020: 62). In algorithmic management, the design and execution of tasks are separate, as in Taylorism. However, unlike in Taylorism, communication is not oriented to clarify to the worker what to do, how to do it and in how much time. Instead, the communication between workers and algorithmic management aims to establish specific power and dependence relationships.

Relations of Power and Dependence

Algorithms can be described as technologies of power insofar as they 'materialize the needs, desires, and aspirations of their owners and enable or constrain multiple forms of agency' (Curchod et al. 2020: 668). Algorithmic management realizes these conditions in various ways, giving rise to various types of power and dependency relationships between workers and management. This power manifests in relations of control and sanctions and in the ability to mould and transform workers' behaviour.

Monitoring and Control

A new version of panoptic power emerges between workers and management due to the information system's continuous supervision of the individual (Galière 2020: 367). One key feature of Artificial Intelligence algorithms in monitoring is their ability to analyse and process massive amounts of heterogeneous data about workers' actions, behaviours or performance automatically and rapidly. AI-driven algorithmic monitoring thus allows a vast array of new information and metrics to be collected and recorded, such as emotions, movements, physical and health conditions, social media activity, stress levels, posture, ergonomics and safety threats during work, real-time desk usage and cognitive or physical employees' engagement in their work (Parent-Rocheleau and Parker 2022: 4). In platform management, monitoring employees is crucial to provide consistent consumer service. For example, Uber can tell a customer when the requested car will arrive because it knows the driver's location in real time.

Algorithms not only mediate the relationships between consumers, platforms and workers but also shape them through their ability to organize the information they receive from all users. Customer ratings are at the heart of the worker coordination and control mechanism (Stark and Pais 2020: 56). Algorithmic management outsources to customers worker performance appraisal and service quality control tasks and responsibilities (Rosenblat and Stark 2016: 3771). This outsourcing places customers in the position of agents in the management loop so that it is the customers and not the organization's managers whom workers must please and whose orders they must follow (Wood et al. 2019: 61). In this way, platforms use consumers' collaboration (which is real unpaid work) to supervise the workers who provide services to them through the platform to their advantage.

Moulding and Transformation

The power imbalance between consumers and workers is clear: workers must please clients or risk heavy penalties; in contrast, consumers can make their assessment without responsibility for its veracity, timeliness or consequences. This management system places workers in a precarious situation by granting clients control over workers with virtually zero accountability for their actions (Maffie 2022: 349–50). Some studies (Cameron and Rahman 2022: 39) suggest that client abuse of workers, including wage stealing and verbal assaults, is higher in platform environments than in other service environments.

The externalization of ratings provides platforms with a mechanism to discipline workers, i.e. to mould and even transform their behaviour. The fact that the rating given by users can be readily aggregated and translated into a ranking is crucial for algorithmic management. While a rating consists of judging something as better or worse than a standard, a ranking arises from assessing something as better or worse than another, even when the ranking has been built without any direct comparison between agents (Stark and Pais 2020: 57). All rating and ranking systems reward certain styles or behaviours over others. Uber, for example, says it sets no rules and leaves drivers free to interact spontaneously with users. However, in practice, they encourage the type of interaction that is best rated (Rosenblat and Stark 2016: 3772). Consequently, these behaviours become mandatory for drivers who want to be positively evaluated.

Nevertheless, the ability of algorithms to monitor and shape behaviour is limited. There are limits to the platforms' ability to control. The effectiveness of monitoring and control mechanisms depends on workers' need or willingness to accept the system's rules. Indeed, not all workers are in the same situation of dependence on the algorithm. Juliet Schor (2021: 45–56) highlights the distinction between 'dependent earners', i.e. workers who earn most or all their income through the platform, and 'supplemental earners', i.e. those other workers who already have sufficient income through other means. With some exceptions, dependent earners who work full-time on a platform tend to earn low incomes, often below the poverty line. These workers especially fear receiving negative evaluations that may lead to deactivation. In contrast, those with other secured income sources experience participating in platforms as an occasion to achieve additional income, realize a personal aspiration or interact with certain types of people. They see themselves as part-time freelancers, taking up some opportunities if they are attractive or turning them down if they are too burdensome.

The ability of platform workers to manage opportunities more or less effectively explains the existence of significant inequalities in the conditions and outcomes of their work. For example, the income inequality among skilled professionals (designers, accountants, computer scientists) on some platforms is 19 to 1, between the 90th and 10th percentile (Wood et al. 2019: 67). This vast difference is explained not so much by the abundance or scarcity of their professional skills as by the reputation achieved by each one in the system, i.e. thanks to the ability of some workers over others to 'manage the algorithm' so that it gives them enough visibility and prestige to attract customers.

Therefore, many platform workers are developing various strategies to circumvent system control and curry favour with the algorithm, including resistance tactics and emotional labour with clients. Some workers develop interaction tactics with potential customers before accepting a job to ensure a positive evaluation or at least avoid a negative evaluation (Cameron and Rahman 2022: 51). For example, some platform drivers pre-emptively inquire and look for clues about the rating a client will give. Even against company policy, they call customers before picking them up, ostensibly to verify their name, but in reality, to inquire about their destination, which the platform purposefully conceals. Drivers act as if these calls are unmonitored, even though they make them through the app. If they believe a potential customer has an unpleasant attitude, many drivers cancel the trip immediately, intuiting that rude passengers are likelier to give low ratings. They know that drivers are also rated on their cancellation rates and still do so to avoid a low rating from an irate customer. On the other hand, other drivers use the information asymmetry to their advantage: they encourage customers to cancel their trip by citing some excuse or sob story. Since most passengers do not know that this goes against company policy, they comply and cancel.

These experiences suggest that management does not actively monitor worker behaviour constantly, or at least does not take action against them, so workers feel free to bypass platform rules to advance their interests (Curchod et al. 2020: 669). Certainly, continuously updating algorithms to avoid user gambits is an expensive, complex process with an uncertain outcome for companies, as further manipulation is always possible (O'Neil 2017). Thus, managerial control in the platform economy is also deployed in other forms of power.

The Power of Discourse

Aware of the limits of the repressive power of algorithmic control, companies resort to persuasion through the discourse of worker's autonomy and entrepreneurship. Thus, companies try to achieve the same behavioural conformity by this other means. Organizations seek to win the minds and hearts of workers so that they adopt patterns of behaviour consistent with the hyper-meritocratic ideal of justice (Galière 2020: 368–9). This subjectivity management becomes a power strategy by emphasizing the appeal of entrepreneurship, i.e. of the worker's autonomy and the voluntary and flexible nature of their occupation (Roberts and Zietsma 2018: 210–12).

The entrepreneurship discourse highlights the worker's independence and the possibility of earning an income in accordance with their individual effort and success. The platform presents itself as a tool, some help, for workers to organize their work individually. Anyone who wants to undertake a work activity has the platform's doors open to offer their services.

In this discourse, the role of the algorithm is legitimized on the grounds of effectiveness. It is taken for granted that workers share this criterion as their own, as individual entrepreneurs and users of the platform.

However, this discourse is not free of contradictions. A significant contradiction lies in the fact that, on the one hand, the platforms expressly treat workers as self-employed entrepreneurs so that they cannot be considered employees (and therefore with consequent labour rights), but, on the other hand, companies need the behaviour of individuals to conform to established patterns.

Moreover, the discourse of entrepreneurship leads to situations of self-exploitation on the part of 'entrepreneurial' workers. To avoid negative evaluations that lead to demotions and deactivation, they give up part of their income or accept abusive conditions. In order to 'please the algorithm' (Bucher et al. 2021: 52), many workers end up practising 'over-compliance', i.e. exceeding the requirements and conditions set to the point of undervaluing their offer to make it more attractive than that of other workers or service providers (Schor 2021: 115–17). For example, some professionals on Upwork offer to do some jobs for free as a test, or bill for fewer hours than they have actually spent on a home repair, or charge a lower rate than they are entitled to for their professional qualifications, to achieve a positive evaluation by the consumer or to avoid a negative evaluation.

Algorithmic management techniques offer workers high flexibility, autonomy, task variety and complexity. Workers can organize themselves as they prefer as long as they meet the results that satisfy the algorithm. So do those who offer legal services, customer service, tech support, web research, animation, logo design, video production, ad posting, telemarketing, academic writing and software development on platforms like Freelancer, Fiverr and many others. However, algorithmic control also results in low pay, social isolation, irregular working hours, overwork, sleep deprivation and exhaustion (Wood et al. 2019: 68). As the platforms allow access to anyone who wants to offer their services, fierce competition arises, pushing down the remuneration and working conditions.

Notwithstanding, the frustration and anxiety experienced by workers is not due to fierce competition, but to the sensation of dealing with machines rather than people, and therefore not being able to communicate and account for their actions (Roberts and Zietsma 2018: 214). A study among telecommunications salespeople (Pachidi et al. 2021: 25–31) found that employees' frustration of having to follow algorithmic recommendations was mainly due to the inexplicability of these recommendations.

On the contrary, some studies have found that algorithmic feedback increases workers' productivity when displaying performance ratings that rely on transparent data and are understandable to workers (Parent-Rocheleau and Parker 2022: 6). Besides, unlike platform companies, where algorithmic systems are central, in traditional organizational settings, the role of algorithms in management is more varied and often limited to helping the individual in managerial tasks such as payroll calculation or recruitment. In these cases, algorithmic systems do not aim to control human behaviour but help workers do their jobs more effectively (Noponen et al. 2023: 5).

In short, algorithmic management configures relations with workers as relations of power and dependence. At this point, the question that arises from a moral point of view is whether this type of management is manipulative: does it use workers as mere means to managers' ends without assessing the moral quality of those ends? As we have seen, compared to traditional management, algorithmic management exacerbates information asymmetries and dependency relationships between employees and managers. In addition, and above all, algorithmic management is different from human management in the impossibility of dialogue, shared deliberation or rational discussion with employees about purposes, goals, objectives, success criteria. Management by algorithms is based on criteria of effectiveness and tends to ignore the criteria of excellence that arise from rational deliberation among practitioners.

The practice–institution tension, according to MacIntyre, consists precisely in the need to negotiate which type of good has priority in each situation and circumstance. Management by algorithms makes such negotiation impossible, or at least much more difficult, as algorithmic calculation imposes the criteria of effectiveness, disregarding considerations of excellence. The next section explores this topic in more detail.

The Price of Effectiveness

Algorithmic management improves the effectiveness of the operations and processes that it coordinates. There is no doubt about this. This improvement derives from measuring correlations between variables to establish performance patterns. These patterns enable the achievement of better results. So, algorithms help carriers optimize delivery routes, bankers improve loan default ratios and designers propose the most acceptable designs to their audiences.

However, these improvements come at a price: they set aside the criteria of excellence in favour of the goods of effectiveness.

Alternatively, to put it provokingly, they define the criteria of excellence in terms of effectiveness and thus denaturalize excellence itself. In some jobs, such as transportation, this confusion does not seem very harmful, and can even be considered positive. In other professions, however, identifying excellence and effectiveness can be catastrophic. MacIntyre's (2011: 324–6) valuation of the recent evolution of universities is a conspicuous example of this. In recent decades, universities in the UK (and in most countries) have undergone frequent assessment processes with the stated aim of ensuring and improving their quality.

These quality evaluation processes of university education were set in motion because of the need to make decisions in an increasingly complex context. Over recent decades, the number of universities and research groups has grown considerably. Educational authorities must make decisions about the approval and funding of institutions and the accreditation of their scholars. Besides, potential students and their families need information to choose the university they want to attend. Rankings that order from best to worst, the universities, each of their schools, and also their individual researchers have emerged to help authorities and families. These rankings seek to offer precise information to their users, drawing on quantitative criteria such as the number of publications in prestigious journals or the funds raised from public and private sources. It is assumed that the higher a university ranks, the greater its quality and, therefore, the greater the return on the investment that authorities and students make. Thus, universities are increasingly perceived in terms of an input–output model, and the ranking function is to predict a particular type of outcome (MacIntyre 2011: 327). Academic work, therefore, is defined in terms of, and subordinated to, external ends such as obtaining a high position in rankings, achieving job placement of graduates, and other supposedly objective quality indicators.

MacIntyre's critique of how money and power have come to tyrannize modern life applies perfectly here: judgements about the 'quality' of academic work cannot be 'objective' in this way, nor can they be reduced to a quantitative measure. According to MacIntyre (2011: 323–9), some goods external and incidental to the practices of academic teaching and research – goods such as the training of skilled workers, research in medicine and contribution to economic growth – can be taken by authorities as goals to be achieved as cost-effectively as possible. However,

> with respect to the goods of the mind, the goods of the understanding and the imagination, the goods internal to the practice of academic teaching and enquiry, for the most part (academic authorities and scholars alike) are either silent or they babble.
>
> (MacIntyre 2011: 324)

The problem is that many academics are

> unable to counterpose to the conception of work presupposed by the educational bureaucrats an adequate rival conception of how academic teaching and enquiry should be evaluated, of what good work at teaching and enquiry consists in. For they too lack an effective shared conception of the academic common good.
>
> (MacIntyre 2011: 328)

The possibility of doing good work in universities is threatened by the process of assimilation from the academic to the bureaucratic, that is, from excellence to effectiveness. This process is increasingly complex but, at the same time, ever less credible since, after all, the algorithmic calculations that generate the rankings are based on judgements made by small groups of referees, pressured by the dynamics of artificially created markets (Sayers 2011: 92). Ultimately, educational authorities and students have information to make effective decisions, but the value of excellence has vanished from that information. Students are regarded as consumers of a service whose quality is judged in terms of return on investment. Faculty and staff of academic institutions are evaluated for their contribution to that outcome. Undoubtedly, students and faculty can cultivate excellence in their disciplines, but only if this does not hinder the achievement of the main objectives that now legitimize the institution.

Algorithmic management intensifies the manipulative tendency of organizations to subordinate excellence to effectiveness. Another illustrative example is that of Spotify, the well-known platform for music streaming. It helps artists, even niche artists, to be on the playlist of a broad public, thus connecting workers and consumers. The platform helps artists access external goods, like income and reputation, thanks to algorithms that use ratings and rankings. This algorithmic evaluation encourages artists to imitate the highest-rated styles, even if they do not meet the highest standards of musical quality. The fact that rankings are based on quantitative measures threatens the way the internal goods of the practice supposedly sustained through Spotify are pursued (namely, the practice of composing music). The platform helps music from all over the world, as well as niche music, to be listened to and receive public support. On the other hand, artists know that, in a way, they are monitored. They receive more visibility and economic rewards only if a listener stays on the track for at least 30 seconds. This has a direct influence on how artists perform their work. They are encouraged to make music that captures the listeners and induces them to stay more than 30 seconds on the track, even if it means giving up better musical arrangements. This 30-second rule is a kind of power structure which is imposed by the platform, and artists must decide whether to abide by these rules or not. However, if they do not conform to this rule, their visibility can be heavily affected, so the mere chance of making a living as an artist can be compromised. In this way, the power of the algorithm to monitor and sanction artists shapes the style of the songs to fit the criteria by which the algorithm calculates the ranking.

Artists have to make decisions about whether or not to optimize their content to best suit the hidden criteria of the platform (Morris 2021: 745). These decisions inevitably take time and thought away from content creation. Moreover, the need for visibility privileges a mode of production that places the technical challenges of discoverability at the centre of the creative process, possibly at the expense of other ways of conceiving and creating cultural goods (p. 746).

In this kind of system, it is the algorithm that decides what is valuable and what is not. Paradoxically, if the digital content people create is seen as valuable by the system, then the system's users also become 'used by the system' (Baskerville et al. 2020: 9). Singers, like university professors (and for that matter, painters, designers, farmers and many other types of practitioners), are valued, not by criteria of excellence according to their communal traditions, but by criteria of effectiveness in their respective markets.

In short, algorithmic management affects the very possibility of doing a good job by overshadowing excellence with effectiveness. Algorithms' ability to find correlations, predict outcomes and generate solutions leaves no room for shared deliberation by human beings on what ends are worth pursuing and for what reasons. Algorithms thus stand as instruments of manipulative relationships between those who manage the algorithms and those whom the algorithm manages.

The question that seems inevitable is whether we want to live in a world increasingly orchestrated by an ever more sophisticated set of algorithms that establishes what kind of work we do, what songs we listen to, which universities are the best, who can get a mortgage (and who cannot), what results we get in our internet searches and what commercials we are allowed to see. Examining this non-neutral performativity of technological developments for workplaces and society at large implies an ethical dimension that is hugely important. This examination may well start posing the question of 'what makes it worthwhile to work and to work well' (MacIntyre 2011: 323) in our technological era. MacIntyre's response would probably be similar to what he proposed in the context of advanced capitalist societies, that the work we do may produce genuine goods to which we contribute personally and responsibly and for which we are rewarded so that we can achieve the goods of the family and community. Hopefully, this answer will illuminate our way to resist the power of algorithms and our search for excellence in our work and in our lives.

References

Baskerville, R. L., Myers, M. D. and Yoo, Y. (2020), 'Digital First: The Ontological Reversal and New Challenges for Information Systems Research', *MIS Quarterly*, 44 (2): 509–23. https://doi.org/10.25300/MISQ/2020/14418

Beadle, R. and Knight, K. (2012), 'Virtue and Meaningful Work', *Business Ethics Quarterly*, 22 (2): 433–50.

Blackledge, P. (2023), 'After Virtue, Managers and Business Ethics', in T. P. S. Angier (ed.), *MacIntyre's After Virtue at 40*, 239–57, Cambridge: Cambridge University Press.

Blackledge, P. and Raptis, B. K. (2020), 'MacIntyre and Marxism', in R. Beadle and G. Moore (eds), *Learning from MacIntyre*, 140–62, Eugene, OR: Pickwick Publications.

Bucher, E. L., Schou, P. K. and Waldkirch, M. (2021), '"Pacifying" the Algorithm: Anticipatory Compliance in the Face of Algorithmic Management in the Gig Economy', *Organization* 28 (1): 44–67. https://doi.org/10.1177/1350508420961531/

Cameron, L. D. and Rahman, H. (2022), 'Expanding the Locus of Resistance: Understanding the Co-constitution of Control and Resistance in the Gig Economy', *Organization Science*, 33 (1): 38–58. https://doi.org/10.1287/orsc.2021.1557

Curchod, C., Patriotta, G., Cohen, L. and Neysen, N. (2020), 'Working for an Algorithm: Power Asymmetries and Agency in Online Work

Settings', *Administrative Science Quarterly*, 65 (3): 644–76. https://doi.org/10.1177/0001839219867024

Cutolo, D., Hargadon, A. and Kenney, M. (2021), 'Competing on Platforms', *MIT Sloan Management Review*, Special Collection New Strategies for the Platform Economy, 1–9.

Daugherty, P. R. and Wilson, H. J. (2018), *Human+Machine: Reimagining Work in the Age of AI*, Boston, MA: Harvard Business Review Press.

Davenport, T. H. and Miller, S. M. (2022), *Working with AI: Real Stories of Human–Machine Collaboration*, Cambridge, MA: The MIT Press.

Galière, S. (2020), 'When Food-Delivery Platform Workers Consent to Algorithmic Management: A Foucauldian Perspective', *New Technology, Work and Employment*, 35 (3): 357–70. https://doi.org/10.1111/ntwe.12177

Heidegger, M. (1993), 'The Question Concerning Technology', in D. F. Krell (ed.), *Basic Writings*, 307–41, New York: Harper.

Kinowska, H. and Sienkiewicz, Ł. J. (2022), 'Influence of Algorithmic Management Practices on Workplace Well-Being–Evidence from European Organizations, *Information Technology & People*, 36 (8): 21–42. https://doi.org/10.1108/ITP-02-2022-0079

Knight, K. (2008), 'After Tradition?: Heidegger or MacIntyre, Aristotle and Marx', *Analyse & Kritik*, 30 (1): 33–52. https://doi.org/10.1515/auk-2008-0103

Knight, K. (2017), 'MacIntyre's Critique of Management', in A. J. Sison and I. Ferrero (eds), *Handbook of Virtue Ethics in Business and Management*, 79–87, New York: Springer.

MacIntyre, A. (1988), *Whose Justice? Which Rationality?* Notre Dame, IN: University of Notre Dame Press. https://doi.org/10.2307/j.ctv1bvnf11

MacIntyre, A. (2007), *After Virtue: A Study in Moral Theory*, Notre Dame, IN: University of Notre Dame Press.

MacIntyre, A. (2008), What More Needs to Be Said? A Beginning, although Only a Beginning, at Saying It, *Analyse & Kritik*, 30 (1): 261–81. https://doi.org/10.1515/auk-2008-0116

MacIntyre, A. (2011), 'Where We Were, Where We Are, Where We Need to Be', in P. Blackledge and K. Knight (eds), *Virtue and Politics: Alasdair MacIntyre's Revolutionary Aristotelianism*, 307–34, Notre Dame, IN: University of Notre Dame Press.

MacIntyre, A. (2016), *Ethics in the Conflicts of Modernity: An Essay on Desire, Practical Reasoning, and Narrative*, Cambridge: Cambridge University Press.

Maffie, M. D. (2022), 'The Perils of Laundering Control through Customers: A Study of Control and Resistance in the Ride-Hail Industry', *ILR Review*, 75 (2): 348–72. https://doi.org/10.1177/0019793920972679

Mardosas, E. (2020), 'Human Flourishing and Labour: Aristotle, MacIntyre, and Marx', in A. Bielskis, E. Leontsini and K. Knight (eds), *Virtue Ethics and*

Contemporary Aristotelianism: Modernity, Conflict, and Politics, 208–21, London: Bloomsbury.

Marx, K. ([1932] 2009), *The Economic and Philosophic Manuscripts of 1844 and the Communist Manifesto*, New York: Prometheus Book.

Möhlmann, M., Zalmanson, L., Henfridsson, O. and Gregory, R. W. (2021), 'Algorithmic Management of Work on Online Labor Platforms: When Matching Meets Control', *MIS Quarterly*, 45 (4): 1999–2022. https://doi.org/10.25300/misq/2021/15333

Moore, G. (2017), *Virtue at Work: Ethics for Individuals, Managers, and Organizations*, Oxford: Oxford University Press.

Moore, G. and Beadle, R. (2006), 'In Search of Organizational Virtue in Business: Agents, Goods, Practices, Institutions and Environments', *Organization Studies*, 27 (3): 369–89. https://doi.org/10.1177/0170840606062427

Morris, J. W. (2021), 'Infrastructures of Discovery: Examining Podcast Ratings and Rankings', *Cultural Studies*, 35 (4–5): 728–49. https://doi.org/10.1080/09502386.2021.1895246

Noponen, N., Feshchenko, P., Auvinen, T., Luoma-aho, V. and Abrahamsson, P. (2024), 'Taylorism on Steroids or Enabling Autonomy? A Systematic Review of Algorithmic Management', *Management Review Quarterly*, 74: 1–27. https://doi.org/10.1007/s11301-023-00345-5

O'Neil, C. (2017), *Weapons of Math Destruction: How Big Data Increases Inequality and Threatens Democracy*, Harmondsworth: Penguin.

Pachidi, S., Berends, H., Faraj, S. and Huysman, M. (2021), 'Make Way for the Algorithms: Symbolic Actions and Change in a Regime of Knowing', *Organization Science*, 32 (1): 18–41. https://doi.org/10.1287/orsc.2020.1377

Parent-Rocheleau, X. and Parker, S. K. (2022), 'Algorithms as Work Designers: How Algorithmic Management Influences the Design of Jobs', *Human Resource Management Review*, 32 (3): 100838. https://doi.org/10.1016/j.hrmr.2021.100838

Roberts, A. and Zietsma, C. (2018), 'Working for an App: Organizational Boundaries, Roles, and Meaning of Work in the "On-Demand" Economy', *Research in the Sociology of Organizations*, 57 (October): 195–225. https://doi.org/10.1108/S0733-558X20180000057008

Rodriguez-Lluesma, C., García-Ruiz, P. and Pinto-Garay, J. (2021), 'The Digital Transformation of Work: A Relational View', *Business Ethics, the Environment & Responsibility*, 30 (1): 157–67. https://doi.org/10.1111/beer.12323

Rosenblat, A. and Stark, L. (2016), 'Algorithmic Labor and Information Asymmetries: A Case Study of Uber's Drivers', *International Journal of Communication*, 10: 3758–84. http://dx.doi.org/10.2139/ssrn.2686227

Sayers, S. (2011), 'MacIntyre and Modernity', in P. Blackledge and K. Knight (eds), *Virtue and Politics: Alasdair MacIntyre's Revolutionary Aristotelianism*, 307–34, Notre Dame, IN: University of Notre Dame Press.

Schor, J. (2021), *After the Gig: How the Sharing Economy Got Hijacked and How to Win It Back*, Oakland, CA: University of California Press.

Sinnicks, M. (2018), 'Leadership after Virtue: MacIntyre's Critique of Management Reconsidered, *Journal of Business Ethics*, 147 (4): 735–46. https://doi.org/10.1007/s10551-016-3381-6

Stark, D. and Pais, I. (2020), 'Algorithmic Management in the Platform Economy', *Sociologica*, 14 (3) 14: 47–72. https://doi.org/10.6092/issn.1971-8853/12221

Vallor, S. (2015), 'Moral Deskilling and Upskilling in a New Machine Age: Reflections on the Ambiguous Future of Character', *Philosophy & Technology*, 28 (1): 107–24. https://doi.org/10.1007/s13347-014-0156-9

Wood, A. J., Graham, M., Lehdonvirta, V. and Hjorth, I. (2019), 'Good Gig, Bad Gig: Autonomy and Algorithmic Control in the Global Gig Economy', *Work, Employment and Society*, 33 (1): 56–75. https://doi.org/10.1177/0950017018785616

4

'Mild Preparations'

Work, Practices and the Internal Good of Recognition

Matthew Sinnicks, Efuntomi Wosu and Craig Reeves

Introduction

This chapter seeks to articulate the ethically developmental potential of work, both in terms of the intrinsic satisfactions of the very best activities, and because of the recognition structures work can provide. We do so by exploring the goods of work in the context of the discussion concerning technological unemployment. One response to the possibility of technological unemployment is provided by the anti-work perspective, the plausibility of which rests in large part on its capacity to do justice to the impoverished nature of much contemporary work. Drawing on MacIntyre's concept of practices we argue, however, that the concept of good work is better equipped to sustain the recognition structures that facilitate the achievement of excellence in those practices. Thus, good work can be viewed, somewhat ironically, as being powerfully conducive to our efforts to prepare ourselves for a world in which leisure is more socially central.

An Age of Leisure?

Recent forecasts about technological changes in the workplace have given new impetus to the idea that a world without work is something humankind might feasibly be able to work towards (see Danaher 2017, 2019; Fleming 2015; Frayn 2015; Weeks 2011, etc.). While it is difficult to predict precisely how disruptive impending technological developments will be, it is clear they will be significant (Floridi 2017: 2). Any form of employment in which people perform standardized or routine tasks is likely to be at risk. Indeed, some have predicted that non-menial jobs will be at risk (Ford 2015: ch. 4), and even some forms of work now regarded as highly skilled and professional, such as some of those involved in the practice of law (Susskind and Susskind 2022) and medicine (Kazzazi 2021).

Clearly, there is nothing inevitable about technology liberating us from tedious labour, but nor is it inevitable that technological innovation will lead to misery. Nevertheless, the issue of how to respond is a pressing one. Yet, this issue of how we would do in a world in which most work now done as a matter of paid employment is unnecessary is not new. Indeed, the anti-work view – which suggests that the most appropriate response is to aim for a world without work – has an extensive history (see Black 1986; Gorz 1985; Granter 2009; Rifkin 2004; Russell 2004 [1935]). According to this view, work is typically characterized by a number of important ills, which mean that we would be better off in a world without work. Such ills are familiar enough, and include boredom (Svendsen 2015), domination (Anderson 2017), exploitation (Faraci 2019), a focus on trivialities that waste human talent (Sinnicks 2022: 55) and no doubt many others.

Writing in 1930, J. M. Keynes perceived the looming possibility of what he referred to as an 'age of leisure', long before AI could be seen as its most notable precondition. However, while much of the anti-work tradition regards the liberation from work as unambiguously good – as Black puts it 'Work is the source of nearly all the misery in the world ... In order to stop suffering, we have to stop working' (1986: 17) – Keynes also saw the personal ethical challenges such an era would impose, an issue not always properly grasped by the anti-work view.

According to Keynes 'the economic problem, the struggle for subsistence' (2015: 81) has always been the most pressing problem facing humankind, and yet this problem will soon be solved. This prospect gives rise to the following question: 'If the economic problem is solved, mankind will be deprived of its traditional purpose ... must we not expect a general "nervous breakdown"?' (2015: 81–2). The central reason to expect this breakdown is the alienating nature of contemporary work, indeed, the ethical impoverishment of contemporary society:

> there is no country and no people, I think, who can look forward to the age of leisure and of abundance without a dread. For we have been trained too long to strive and not enjoy. It is a fearful problem for the ordinary person, with no special talents, to occupy himself, especially if he no longer has roots in the soil or in custom or in the beloved conventions of a traditional society.
>
> (2015: 83)

The notion that people, in contemporary society, all too often have no roots in the soil or in the conventions of traditional society is a familiar one, and has affinities with a variety of critiques of contemporary society, including those offered by Taylor (1989), Sennett (1998), and above all, MacIntyre (2007), whose work we return to below.

Nevertheless, the prospect of an age of leisure gives us some grounds for hope. According to Keynes, 'We shall be able to rid ourselves of many of the pseudo-moral principles which have hag-ridden us for two thousand years, by which we have exalted some of the most distasteful of human qualities into the position of the highest virtues' (2015: 83). If we can rid ourselves of this misconception '[w]e shall once more value ends above means and prefer the good to the useful' (2015: 85) and be in a position to turn our attention to truly valuable things and genuine virtues.

While this liberation may be, to say the least, some way off, in the meantime 'there will be no harm in making mild preparations for our destiny, in encouraging, and experimenting in, the arts of life as well as the activities of purpose' (2015: 85). This is an intuitively appealing thought, for it highlights the contrast between living and working, activity that is its own end and activity that is instrumental to external ends – a contrast that's embedded in the fabric of our existing social world. The market, so the story goes, encourages experimentation in the instrumental activities of purpose. But not necessarily the 'arts of life'. In fact, the experimentally guided progress of the division of labour often seems to come into direct conflict with experimentation in the 'arts of life', as where increasingly rationalized production processes result in increasingly simplified and mechanized work roles.

While the production of material and cultural products has, through experimentation, become more efficient, arguably, the scope of experimentation for the worker in their work and the consumer in their free time has diminished. In this light, Keynes's proposal is a timely call to refocus our priorities on, to borrow Mill's phrase, 'experiments in living' (Mill 1989: *passim*) rather than producing, since the market often caters well to experimentation in the latter but frequently at the expense of the former. If we can anticipate at some point reclaiming our human existence from the tyranny of necessity, we would do well to pre-emptively cultivate our at-present suppressed capacities for living.

The Arts of Life and the Question of Work

That we might, without work, be liberated to use our free time to pursue meaningful activities is a central thought in the anti-work tradition. Consider, for example, this passage from Gorz:

> As the periods of disposable time become longer, non-working time can become something other than the obverse of working time … the counterpart of a work which, by its monotony, is anaesthetizing and exhausting. As disposable time increases, it becomes both possible and necessary to find other activities and relations to structure it … It becomes possible for … a new societal and cultural space, composed of autonomous activities with freely chosen ends, to be opened up.
>
> (Gorz 1989: 92)

Gorz here attempts to highlight the need for structures that might help us deal with Keynes' plausible worry that the impoverishment of our work-world undermines our capacity for free enjoyment in deeper ways that may not be so easy to shake off, perhaps leaving us ill-equipped to deal with the apparent freedom of a hypothetical 'age of leisure'.

Gorz's talk of the 'multi-activity society' (1999: *passim*; see also Granter and Aroles 2023) is part of a rich heritage of visions of a better society. It tacitly reflects a dissatisfaction with alienating work, which Marx expressed in his early writings (Marx 1978: 70–81; see also Bielskis 2023), and clearly has an affinity with Marx and Engel's characterization of a communist society, outlined in *The German Ideology*:

> where nobody has one exclusive sphere of activity but each can become accomplished in any branch he wishes, society regulates the general production and thus makes it possible for me to do one thing today and another tomorrow, to hunt in the morning, fish in the afternoon, rear cattle in the evening, criticise after dinner, just as I have a mind, without ever becoming hunter, fisherman, herdsman or critic.
>
> (Marx and Engels 1970: 54)

It is no accident that Marx and Engels appeal to leisure activities of the elite class – hunting, engagement with the arts – in their description of a better world. The better world grants everyone the freedom to pursue those activities which are clearly enjoyable and appealing.

Gorz's vision also has important connections to MacIntyre's thought, again in at least two senses. Firstly, it aligns with MacIntyre's critique of modernity insofar as the world of work is dominated by the imperatives of the market. For MacIntyre, 'what is essentially human is rational activity, and consumption exists to serve activity and not to be served by it. We ought to eat in order to work, not vice versa' (MacIntyre 1979: 44) On this view, human purpose is not only geared towards survival or consumption, but to richer activity. This stands in stark contrast to the reality of the contemporary workplace, in which most people have a 'treadmill of a job' (MacIntyre 2015: 18). Such jobs are not merely bad in themselves but they also tend to serve a broader system in which production is devised to meet untutored consumer preferences. Indeed, in some ways the 'age of leisure' seems to be a prerequisite for the freedoms needed to reverse the ethical deficiencies of modernity. This is because it would allow room for engagement in MacIntyrean practices, which brings us to the second aspect of the vision of a 'multi-activity' society with an affinity to MacIntyre's thought.

According to MacIntyre's definition, a 'practice' is a:

> coherent and complex form of socially established co-operative human activity through which goods internal to that form of activity are realized in the course of trying to achieve those standards of excellence which are appropriate to, and partially definitive of, that form of activity, with the result that human powers to achieve excellence, and human conceptions of the ends and goods involved, are systematically extended.
>
> (2007: 187)

Perhaps the most important aspect of this definition to bear in mind is that of 'internal goods'. These can be achieved only by engaging in the activity in question, and contrast with 'external goods' such as money, power and reputation, which are 'always some individual's property and possession' (2007: 190), and can always be acquired in a variety of ways. MacIntyre illustrates this concept of practices with repeated references to 'arts, games, and sciences' (2007: 188, 190, 200). These kinds of activities clearly provide an opportunity to attempt to achieve excellence, to extend our conceptions of the ends and goods involved, in the way that MacIntyre describes. MacIntyre also notes that practices do not have set and stable goals, but rather that 'the goods themselves are transmuted by the history of the activity' (2007: 194). Again, the arts, games and sciences – the sorts of cultural and intellectual activities which we might choose to partake in if liberated from work in a multi-activity society – seem to be apt illustrations here. Those who excel at such activities do so in a way that is in dialogue with the master–practitioners of the past, and MacIntyre invokes Rembrandt, Bartok, J. M. W. Turner and W. G. Grace as examples of such master–practitioners. Thus, it is unsurprising that MacIntyre's most evocative descriptions of practices focus on chess (2007: 188), when discussing induction into a practice, and portrait painting (2007: 189), when discussing the historical development of practices.

Because practices, in MacIntyre's sense, are clearly rich and engaging in a way that the sort of leisure activities needed to cope with the monotony and exhaustion of contemporary work, to recall Gorz's characterization, it seems that MacIntyre's thought is well placed to contribute to the anti-work tradition's conversation about the shape of an age of leisure. We can readily see how MacIntyrean practices might promote communities where people learn, reason, cultivate friendships and indeed pursue any number of the other things we might want from a world without work.

However, this is not to say that MacIntyre should be understood as part of the anti-work tradition. MacIntyre's discussion of practices also includes a range of kinds of work, such as farming and commercial fishing, and indeed has sometimes been thought to offer an understanding of what work might be at its best (Keat 2008; Muirhead 2004). As such, it has been applied to many forms of work beyond those rather exclusive domains of arts, games and sciences. These include circus (Beadle 2013; Beadle and Sinnicks 2024), business (Bernacchio and Couch 2023; Moore 2002), management (Beabout 2012), software design (Bolade-Ogunfodun et al. 2022) and financial trading (Rocchi et al. 2021).

MacIntyre clearly regards work as being of great ethical significance. MacIntyre suggests that 'there is a close connection between being a good human being and doing good work', a connection that 'has been lost sight of altogether in the contemporary workplace' (2011: 323). Indeed, for MacIntyre, work, when in good order, should be 'thought of as a kind of prayer and performed as an act of prayer' (2011: 323).

Despite this, there remains a sense in which MacIntyre's concept of practices is bifurcated between a description of rich, rewarding, morally educative activities, that ultimately has very little to do with *work*, and a conception of the goods of (ordinary) work understood primarily in terms of practice-based communities. The chess-playing child in *After Virtue* has no need to turn professional to gain the benefits of engaging in chess, while the fishing crew risking their lives at sea, in MacIntyre's reply essay in *After MacIntyre* (MacIntyre 1994: 284–6), would have to be understood very differently if they were doing it for fun.

Indeed, if we are forced to choose between practices that might be understood as belonging to the category of 'noble leisure' (chess, music, etc.), which is clearly quite distinct from mere relaxation, and the practices that constitute examples of somewhat prosaic work, it seems entirely reasonable to prefer the former. The dangerous task facing the commercial fishing crew, the often tiring and sometimes tedious work of the farmer, clearly possess less intrinsic appeal than the leisure activities chosen largely because of that appeal. The internal goods of such leisure activities, not to mention the possibilities for a systematic extension of the ends and goods involved, are plain. As a result, the anti-work tradition seems well placed to withstand a MacIntyrean defence of work, in part because of the resources provided by MacIntyre's own account of practices.

Indeed, forms of work which are practices seem particularly geared towards those whose focus remains on preserving or cultivating 'roots in the soil or in custom or in the beloved conventions of a traditional society' (Keynes 2015: 83). If we really think that such forms of work are liable to become less necessary in future, thus allowing us to focus on the 'good' rather than the 'useful', it becomes increasingly difficult to imagine an argument in favour of human beings risking their lives at sea in order to catch fish simply because doing so is a practice, when many other practices, which are less dangerous and more amenable to a creative engagement that allows for an extension of our understanding of the ends and goods involved, are available within the multi-activity society.

We noted above that it would be wrong to categorize MacIntyre as an anti-work theorist. But does this observation mean that MacIntyre *should* support an anti-work position? Not necessarily. And the reason for this is that there is an additional facet of work, of serious and devoted engagement in practices in a manner that seems intuitively distinct from leisure, that demands consideration: recognition.

Recognition as an Internal Good

In this section, we aim to cast a certain kind of recognition as a good internal to practices. Recognition is clearly a very important good. As Bernacchio puts it, 'Recognition is a fundamental good within human life, whereby one's status as a person becomes tangible and real' (Bernacchio 2023: 2). It is clearly an important good of work (Dejours et al. 2018; Gheaus and Herzog 2016).

In addition to being important, recognition is also a multifaceted concept. Recognition per se, that is, recognition in the broadest sense, attaches to persons *qua* persons, and thus stands outside the basic categories of goods internal and external to practices. This is the sense of 'recognition' that has been central to contemporary political philosophical debates (see, for instance, Taylor 1994). But more local kinds of recognition can be achieved in a wide range of ways. As such, it is not internal to any particular practice, and may perhaps be best understood as an external good, on MacIntyre's schema, like money or reputation. If someone fails to achieve recognition in one domain, they can achieve it in another. Imagine an unsuccessful farmer turned master stand-up comic. Recognition is not forthcoming in the domain of failure, but is in the domain of mastery.

However, there are also fine-grained differences between such examples of recognition that allow us to understand recognition as an internal good as well. Consider examples such as the professional tennis player obsessed with winning, or the physicist obsessed with being promoted. Such figures appear to be focused on external goods: victory and an increase in status appear to be achievable in a variety of ways, and thus not internal to any particular practice. And this is, of course, a real possibility. Nevertheless, there is a range of forms such aspirations may take, including a desire for victory or status that is best analysed in terms of internal goods.

While it might be hard for an outside observer to discern the difference, a tennis player who is obsessed with victory for its own sake is quite different from a tennis player obsessed with winning at tennis but only as a result of excellent play. There is something very different about a victory achieved as a result of other competitors pulling out through injury and a victory achieved as a result of fairly beating the best players. If, for instance, a physicist is fixated on promotion for its own sake or for the financial benefits that accompany a promotion, then he or she will attempt to obtain it by whatever means necessary, including perhaps those that may seem to be underhand or dubious in some way, e.g. by 'calling in a favour' or agreeing to support a departmental policy they do not agree with. If, by contrast, the physicist is notably determined to be promoted because he or she views it as a marker of their genuine expertise and accomplishments within the field of physics, that is rather a different matter. While any particular individual is liable to self-exculpatory delusions in this regard, in principle, this latter focus on achievement is entirely compatible with a proper focus on internal goods.

Recognition within practices is, when these practices are in good order, intimately related to excellence. As a result, they can in fact be the locus where internal and external goods meet. This is because recognition clearly relates to an external good like reputation, and, in the case of proper recognition within a practice, has at the same time a distinctive quality that cannot be achieved in any other way. The champion tennis player is recognized *qua tennis player*, the deserving physics professor is recognized *qua physics professor*, and neither type of recognition can be achieved outside that particular practice. Nor is it substitutable by a more generic type of recognition. Moreover, it cannot be collapsed into any of the external goods like wider esteem or reputation with which it might typically be connected: no amount of ill-gotten or undeserved external, wider esteem will amount to such proper recognition within the practice. All the celebrity or prestige in the world is still not an objectively adequate substitute for a Grand Slam title or a Nobel Prize won for the right reason, in the right way.

So while it might seem counterintuitive to regard something like recognition as an internal good, since in many ways it is quite distinct from the activity itself, there are several reasons to hold that certain kinds of recognition are better understood as an internal good rather than an external good. Firstly, MacIntyre characterizes external goods as those for which there 'are always alternative ways for achieving such goods, and their achievement is never to be had only by engaging in some particular kind of practice' (2007: 188). To be recognized *qua* tennis player or *qua* physics professor cannot be achieved in any way other than by engaging in tennis or physics. There are no alternative ways of achieving these goods. Secondly, MacIntyre characterizes living a specific kind of life as a distinctive good of portrait painting (2007: 188, 190), and the absence of a specific kind of life as one of the reasons that teaching is not a practice (MacIntyre and Dunne 2002: 9). Again, the specific kind of life one leads as a practitioner is, in some sense, outside the activity that constitutes the practice, and yet cannot be achieved in any other way, just as is the case with 'internal good recognition'.

Recognition in this sense seems to be distinctly more available within contexts we would normally think of as 'work' than contexts we think of as leisure. Within work we are answerable to standards external to ourselves, and not reducible to our own enjoyment or inclination. This does of course apply to very serious amateur pursuit of certain goods, though of course it may make sense to see, for example, the very serious novelist who has yet to secure a book deal, or the very serious physics PhD who has yet to land a post, as engaged in work rather than leisure, in part because they are subjecting themselves to the standards of the practices of literature and physics, over an extended period, rather than enjoying a pleasing pastime.

But there remains an important distinction between those who eventually come to be seen to make such a contribution, and those who, despite their best efforts, do not. The recognition structures of the activity play a central role here. This aspect of practices is clearly bound up with MacIntyre's argument that practices require institutions (2007: 194), and thus that the pursuit of internal goods of practices requires us to secure external goods – power, reputation, money – in support. On this schema, 'recognition' looks somewhat akin to 'reputation', an external good. But again, we can make a further distinction. The full-time tennis player needs an income. He or she could, of course, attempt to support their commitment to a full-time tennis tour through burglary or the establishment of a ponzi-scheme, but much more desirable is to win prize money at tennis tournaments as a result of excellent play.

Our imaginary tennis player clearly needs money, and wants victory and recognition, but not just any victory and recognition, only those that emerge from excellent play and are obtained in the correct way. Recognition from the right people and for the right reason are the sorts of goods that attend only to the practice of tennis. This distinct kind of recognition is a good internal to practice. It is bound up with the standards of excellence internal to that practice, and so ultimately available only from master–practitioners or those otherwise qualified to judge the practice through their intimate familiarity with it. It is not excluded from leisure altogether, as we noted above, even if it is all but unavailable to leisure pursuits that are only engaged in occasionally, for fun. Recognition structures, through which many valuable kinds of internal good recognition are distributed, are often principally managed through work institutions.

To broaden the point so that it might illuminate the broader category of work, one important contrast might be that in the context of leisure taken for mere relaxation, improvement – excellence, virtue – is incidental and ancillary to the pursuit of immediate enjoyment, relaxation or fun, whereas in the serious context the enjoyment and fun is subordinate to and derivative of the pursuit of excellence itself. Where immediate enjoyment is subordinate to the cultivation of excellence and virtue, the concept of work as opposed to leisure is arguably implicated. Those who play sports for leisure do not typically spend most of that time in drills and routines, but rather in playing games, despite the fact that playing competitive games is not necessarily the best way to build excellence. Playing a game of tennis is much more enjoyable, though, than doing endless drills designed to improve individual aspects of one's game, just as playing pieces is much more fun than playing endless scales and arpeggios on a piano.

In genuine practices, when we are encouraging our children to engage in an art, craft, science, etc., we tend to say things like 'if you want to *enjoy* it, you have to *work* at it'. Such language embodies the connection between work, seriousness and excellence. It is in many cases true that excellence is its own reward – that being good at something is much more fulfilling than doing it badly, and becoming good at a genuine practice generally requires serious, diligent and disciplined effort, much of which is not immediately fun. This highlights why the virtue of constancy is so important for MacIntyre (2007: 203, see also Robson 2015), but also why Keynes's distinction between the 'arts of life' and the 'activities of purpose' misses the morally educative role of those activities where life, and a purposiveness better captured with reference to the concept of work, come together.

Indeed, the understanding of a certain kind of recognition as a peculiar kind of internal good can be expanded further. While recognition as an internal good in the arts, games and sciences may be conferred almost exclusively by the particularly well-informed insider or master–practitioner, there are certain practices that contribute to basic human needs so transparently that internal good recognition can be provided by professional accreditation; i.e. a broader form of recognition that can only be achieved through engaging in particular practices, and in no other way, or by the appreciation of the public at large, despite their relative ignorance of the technicalities of the practice. Again such goods are similar to the broader external good of status, but because 'we can only specify them in terms of' the practices in question (MacIntyre 2007: 188), they are best understood as an internal good. Examples of this might include those who work in healthcare (see Reeves and Sinnicks 2023), but also in engineering or aviation, where a 'job well done' is so obviously important to safety that its relationship to human well-being is clear. For the concert pianist, internal good recognition might only be available from a relatively select group of connoisseurs, but the person whose work is a matter of life and death makes a contribution that is more widely comprehensible. As a result, a kind of recognition that attaches to particular roles, and cannot be achieved in any other way, attaches to nurses, doctors, engineers, airline pilots and so on. This recognition is important and essentially connected to the domain of work.

This broader sense in which recognition is an internal good relates to the wider worth or importance of one's excellence for others. This aspect further helps distinguish work from leisure in its internal goods. For even the excellent amateur chess player or poet who receives recognition from peers in the practice will not thereby get a sense of doing something worthwhile that matters to others whether or not they understand it. Athletes and artists find broader recognition insofar as their work is appreciated by non-experts, the wider world, but this is rather contingent. Athletes often seem to feel an obligation to their audience to do well, but little really hinges on their performance. Pilots and nurses are in a different situation. They have to do a good job else people die. Whilst taking pride and finding fulfilment in excellence, in the recognition by peers that they are doing the practice well, that recognition is backed up by a broader recognition of their practice, and of excellence in their practice, as important.

In our society, certain sorts of work naturally attract this kind of recognition because of their critical function in the reproduction of life, but in principle a much wider range of practices could be recognized as of wider worth in a society more oriented to what is worthwhile. But that would not necessarily be a post-work society. It might better be envisaged as a society in which work comes into its own, and recognition as an internal good can be properly realized.

Concluding Remarks

What are we to make of Keynes's prognostications in the light of the preceding discussion? On the one hand, 'mild preparations' for a future of leisure without breakdown would require honing the capacity for enjoyment of what is not mere drudgery. If the capacity for enjoyment of what is internally good also involves work, disciplined devotion with the expectation of an internal reward, and if we are entrenched in a dichotomy of work that requires disciplined effort and leisure enjoyment that ought to be effortless, we will need to re-educate ourselves – through at least 'mild preparations' – in order to appreciate better the ways in which excellence and flourishing require work.

On the other hand, Keynes appears to imagine that his anticipated 'mental breakdown' would flow from the fact that, under the dominance of the market exchange, we are so immersed in activities that are purely instrumental with minimal intrinsic goods, that we would be ill-equipped to tolerate – let alone enjoy – a life of activities that have intrinsic goods, i.e. genuine practices. But we make a mistake if we imagine the aim is to learn to enjoy the internally good activities of genuine practices in the absence of broader recognition of not merely doing something well, but of doing something well that is of wider human worth. Perhaps the mental breakdown Keynes dreads is an artefact of his failure to give proper weight to this latter dimension, the broader recognition we seek from doing something well that makes a positive contribution to the lives of our fellows. To be condemned to cloistered, if intrinsically enjoyable, triviality that is of no worth to others more broadly is understandably an anxiety-inducing prospect.

The vision of an age of leisure risks omitting the internal good of recognition, but it is perhaps for this reason not a very plausible vision. The dread of a mental breakdown beyond drudgery may be assuaged if we shift our vision for a post-drudgery world, away from leisure as such, to an age of good work; this would on this account combine the valuable features of leisure and of work as we know them – internally rewarding practices and the internal good of broader recognition – while jettisoning the bad features of both as we know them (triviality or irrelevance to others, and drudgery). Mild preparations for such an age might be carved out if we were to focus on redeeming the internal goods from the clutches of market etiolation of kinds of work that are most clearly candidates for the unity of internal good and broader recognition.

References

Anderson, E. (2017), *Private Government: How Employers Rule Our Lives (and Why We Don't Talk about It)*, Princeton, NJ: Princeton University Press.

Beabout, G. R. (2012), 'Management as a Domain-relative Practice That Requires and Develops Practical Wisdom', *Business Ethics Quarterly*, 22 (2): 405–32.

Beadle, R. (2013), 'Managerial Work in a Practice-embodying Institution: The Role of Calling, the Virtue of Constancy', *Journal of Business Ethics*, 113 (4), 679–90.

Beadle, R. and Sinnicks, M. (2024), 'It's a Three-ring Circus: How Morally Educative Practices Are Undermined by Institutions', *Business Ethics Quarterly*, 1–27. https://doi.org/10.1017/beq.2024.1

Bernacchio, C. (2023), 'Business and the Ethics of Recognition', *Journal of Business Ethics*, 185 (1): 1–16.

Bernacchio, C. and Couch, R. (2023), 'Value Creation and the Internal Goods of Business', *Frontiers in Sociology*, 7: 980816.

Bielskis, A. (2023), 'Judging Automation: Towards a Normative Critical Theory', *Capital & Class*. https://doi.org/10.1177/03098168231199905

Black, B. (1986), *The Abolition of Work and Other Essays*, Port Townshend, WA: Loompanics Unlimited.

Bolade-Ogunfodun, Y., Sinnicks, M., Akrivou, K. and Scalzo, G. (2022), 'Exploring the Vulnerability of Practice-like Activities: An Ethnographic Perspective', *Frontiers in Sociology*, 7: 1–14.

Danaher, J. (2017), Will Life Be Worth Living in a World without Work?' *Science and Engineering Ethics*, 23 (1): 41–64.

Danaher, J. (2019), *Automation and Utopia*, Cambridge, MA: Harvard University Press.

Dejours, C., Deranty, J. P., Renault, E. and Smith, N. H. (2018), *The Return of Work in Critical Theory*, New York: Columbia University Press.

Faraci, D. (2019), 'Wage Exploitation and the Nonworseness Claim: Allowing the Wrong, to Do More Good', *Business Ethics Quarterly*, 29 (2): 169–88.

Fleming, P. (2015), *The Mythology of Work: How Capitalism Persists Despite Itself*, London: Pluto Press.

Floridi, L. (2017), 'Robots, Jobs, Taxes, and Responsibilities', *Philosophy & Technology*, 30 (1): 1–4.

Ford, M. (2015), *The Rise of Robots*, London: Oneworld Publications.

Frayne, D. (2015), *The Refusal of Work*, London: Zed Books.

Gheaus, A. and Herzog, L. (2016), 'The Goods of Work (Other Than Money!)', *Journal of Social Philosophy*, 47 (1): 70–89.

Gorz, A. (1985), *Paths to Paradise*, London: Pluto Press.

Gorz, A. (1989), *Critique of Economic Reason*, London: Verso.

Gorz, A. (1999), *Reclaiming Work*, Cambridge: Polity.

Granter, E. (2009), *Critical Social Theory and the End of Work*, London: Routledge.

Granter, E. and Aroles, J. (2023), 'Crisis and Utopia: André Gorz and the End of Work', *Journal of Classical Sociology*, 23 (2): 211–28.

Kazzazi, F. (2021), 'The Automation of Doctors and Machines', *Future Healthcare Journal*, 8 (2): e257–e262.

Keat, R. (2008), 'Practices, Firms and Varieties of Capitalism', *Philosophy of Management*, 7 (1): 77–91.

Keynes, J. M. (2015), 'Economic Possibilities for Our Grandchildren', in R. Skidelsky (ed.), *The Essential Keynes*, 75–85, London: Penguin Books.

MacIntyre, A. (1979), 'Social Science Methodology as the Ideology of Bureaucratic Authority', in M. S. Falco (ed.), *Through the Looking Glass: Epistemology and the conduct of Enquiry*, 42–58, Lanham, MD: University Press of America.

MacIntyre, A. (1994), 'A Partial Response to My Critics', in J. Horton and S. Mendus (eds), *After MacIntyre: Critical Perspectives on the Work of Alasdair MacIntyre*, 283–384, Cambridge: Polity Press.

MacIntyre, A. (2007), *After Virtue*, 3rd edn, London: Duckworth.

MacIntyre, A. (2011), 'Where We Were, Where We Are, Where We Need to Be', in P. Blackledge and K. Knight (eds), *Virtue and Politics*, 307–34, Notre Dame, IN: Dame University Press.

MacIntyre, A. (2015), 'The Irrelevance of Ethics', in A. Bielskis and K. Knight (eds), *Virtue and Economy: Essays on Morality and Markets*, 7–21, Farnham: Ashgate.

MacIntyre, A. and Dunne, J. (2002), 'Alasdair MacIntyre on Education: In Dialogue with Joseph Dunne', *Journal of Philosophy of Education*, 36 (1): 1–19.

Marx, K. (1978), 'Economic and Philosophic Manuscripts of 1844', in R. C. Tucker (ed.), *The Marx-Engels Reader*, 2nd edn, 66–125, New York: W. W. Norton.

Marx, K. and Engels, F. (1970), *The German Ideology*, London: Lawrence & Wishart Ltd.

Mill, J. S. (1989), *On Liberty and Other Writings*, Cambridge: Cambridge University Press.

Moore, G. (2002), 'On the Implications of the Practice–Institution Distinction: MacIntyre and the Application of Modern Virtue Ethics to Business', *Business Ethics Quarterly*, 12 (1): 19–32.

Muirhead, R. (2004), *Just Work*, London: Harvard University Press.

Reeves, C. and Sinnicks, M. (2023), 'Needs, Creativity and Care: Adorno and the Future of Work', *Organization*, 30 (5): 851–72.

Rifkin, J. (2004), *The End of Work: The Decline of the Global Labour Force and the Dawn of the Post-Market Era*, new edn, New York: Penguin.

Robson, A. (2015), 'Constancy and Integrity: (Un)measurable Virtues?' *Business Ethics: A European Review*, 24 (S2): 115–29.

Rocchi, M., Ferrero, I. and Beadle, R. (2021), 'Can Finance Be a Virtuous Practice? A MacIntyrean Account', *Business Ethics Quarterly*, 31 (1): 75–105.

Russell, B. (2004), *In Praise of Idleness and Other Essays*, London: Routledge.

Sennett, R. (1998), *The Corrosion of Character*, New York: W. Marx, K. ([1859] 1904), *A Contribution to the Critique of Political Economy*, Chicago: Charles H. Kerr & Company. W. Norton.

Sinnicks, M. (2022), 'On the Analogy between Business and Sport: Towards an Aristotelian Response to the Market Failures Approach to Business Ethics', *Journal of Business Ethics*, 177 (1): 49–61.

Susskind, R. and Susskind, D. (2022), *The Future of the Professions*, updated edn, Oxford: Oxford University Press.

Svendsen, L. (2015), *Work*, 2nd edn, London: Routledge.

Taylor, C. (1989), *Sources of the Self*, Cambridge, MA: Harvard University Press.

Taylor, C. (1994), *Multiculturalism*, expanded paperback edn, Princeton, NJ: Princeton University Press.

Weeks, K. (2011), *The Problem with Work: Feminism, Marxism, Antiwork Politics, and Postwork Imaginaries*, Durham, NC: Duke University Press.

5

A Note on Marx, Alienation and Technology

Ruth Porter Groff

In 'Industrialization and Capitalism in the Work of Max Weber', Marcuse tells us that Weber's discussion of reason, technology and capitalism is flawed in two important ways. The first is that Weber fails to distinguish between '"pure," formal, technical reason' and 'the reason of domination' (Marcuse 1968: 223); the second is that he also fails, in some sense ironically, to appreciate that so-called 'technical reason' is in fact substantive, a bearer of social content. The upshot of these two mistakes, says Marcuse, is that 'technical' reason, as conceived by Weber, is both abstract and necessarily oppressive. For Marcuse, by contrast, 'technical reason' itself is '*historical*' (Marcuse 1968: 225). 'Technology', he writes, 'is always a historical-social *project*: in it is projected what a society and its ruling interests intend to do with men and things' (Marcuse 1968: 224). For this reason (no pun intended), technical reason is neither neutral nor necessarily an instrument of capital accumulation. To quote Marcuse again, 'technical reason is the social reason ruling a given society and can be changed in its very structure. As technical reason, it can become the technique of liberation' (Marcuse 1968: 225). It is against the backdrop of Marcuse's analysis that I want to reflect on the topic at hand. I will start by laying out Marx's views on alienation, then consider what they might imply with respect to technology. In keeping with Marcuse, I take it for granted that 'the machine', as he puts it (Marcuse 1968: 225), bears a social imprint – even machinery that is used for good. As it happens, my Marx is more of an Aristotelian than is Marcuse's. Accordingly, while my aim will be to show how Marx might help us to think about the concern of the present volume, namely, the relationship between human flourishing and automation, I will make some use of Aristotle along the way, if only for heuristic purposes.

Alienation as per Marx

The obvious place to begin in setting out Marx's thinking about alienation, is with the *Economic and Philosophic Manuscripts of 1844*. Some readers of Marx contend that there is what Louis Althusser called an 'epistemic break' between the 1844 work and *Capital*, such that it is only a young, pre-scientific Marx who cares about supposedly 'humanist' concerns such as alienation. Manifestly, the mode of theorizing in *Capital* differs from that of the early manuscripts. But – in my view – the object(s) of inquiry do(es) not. At the centre of *Capital*, too, that is, is the phenomenon of 'estranged labour', as Marx called it in 1844. Consequently, I will attend to both the early and the later treatments of alienation before asking what, if anything, Marx might be able to help us to say about the relationship between automation and human flourishing construed in at least loosely

Aristotelian terms. I am (painfully) aware that I am hardly the first person to think about any of these matters. Ranging from the Marcuse referenced above to others associated with the Frankfurt School, to a host of ecological Marxists, to authors such as Bertell Ollman (Ollman 1971), Amy Wendling (Wendling 2009) and Clive Lawson (Lawson 2017) and others, it is well-traversed ground. My aims are therefore quite modest. I want mainly to demonstrate that and how relevant bits of primary texts pertain to the topic at hand. What is arguably distinctive about my approach is the extent to which I take Marx's thought to intersect with Aristotle's at certain crucial junctures, and – albeit perhaps less so – the continuity that I believe exists at the deepest level between the *1844 Manuscripts* and *Capital*.

In the early manuscripts, Marx says to Hegel that there is a difference between objectification and alienation, or objectification as such and what we might call alienated-objectification. Objectification as such – transposed from objective idealism into Marx's non-reductive materialism – is when we express our embodied subjectivity via the creation of an artefact. Aristotle conceived of this process as one of an artisan imposing a new form upon an existing substance or artefact. The potter who has created a ceramic mug has objectified (Aristotle would say actualized) his or her pottery-making capacity in the now-existent cup, the material cause of which is still clay, but which has come to have a different form than that of unshaped clay. In 1844, Marx used the Hegelian vocabulary of subjects objectifying their subjectivity. But the Aristotelian language shows up in *Capital*, especially when Marx is talking about concrete labouring, so it is worth appreciating that Marx's use of the concept of objectification can be expressed in an Aristotelian register. In contrast to what I am calling objectification as such, alienated-objectification is not mere production, or labouring. It is what Marx in 1844 calls 'estranged labour'.

What is Marx saying when he tells us that labour is 'estranged'? By the term itself, we can take Marx to mean something like 'made foreign to us'; 'related to us in an inappropriate – or, as Aristotle would put it, "perverted" – manner'. Marx mostly leaves it up to us to infer what the nature of *non*-estranged, *non*-alienated labour is, or would be, from the account that we are given of labour that *is* estranged; I will come back to this.

Estranged labour is estranged in four senses, says Marx. First, those who do the labouring neither own nor retain control over the objects of their labour. Thus '[t]he worker', Marx writes, 'is related to the product of his labour as to an alien object' (Marx 1964: 109). Moreover, 'the more the worker spends himself, the more powerful becomes the alien world of objects which he creates over and against himself' (Ibid.: 108). Second, estranged labour is labour in which the very act of producing – the activity itself – has become 'alien', 'external' and foreign to the producer (Ibid.: 110). Such activity is not an expression of the producer's own unfettered creative capacities, says Marx; it 'does not belong to his essential being' (Ibid.: 110). On the contrary, estranged labour is experienced as 'a labour of self-sacrifice, of mortification' (Ibid.: 111). Third, and crucial, estranged labour is alienated in the sense that what has become activity to be 'shunned like the plague', as Marx puts it (Ibid.: 111), never done for its own sake, is nothing less than the capacity for free, self-conscious, creative engagement with nature that is the essence of what it is to be a human being, according to Marx. This monstrous inversion Marx calls alienation from 'species-being' (Ibid.: 114). I will spell out the positive account of species-being in a moment. Finally, estranged labour is alienated in that it occurs in a context within which people are fundamentally disconnected from one another. Above all, this is because – and inasmuch as – some own the means of production while others (namely, those producing objects that are alien to them, and doing so in an alienated way, contrary to the species-appropriate activity that is the 'distinctive endowment', to use J. S. Mill's lovely phrase (Mill 1951: 155–6), of creatures of our kind) do not.

Of these four related aspects of alienation, the third is arguably the most profound. Although it is private ownership of the means of production, by some rather than by all, that underwrites the very possibility of estranged labour, it is the deformation of species-being that is the supreme affront. Why? Because Marx, like Aristotle, has it that the full actualization of our characteristically human powers is the ultimate good for human beings (Groff 2015). Marx, too, distinguishes humans from other animals on the basis of the quality of our consciousness. But Marx, following Rousseau, connects what he, Marx, dubs 'species-being' to the way in which we interact with nature. Other animals engage with nature instinctively, says Rousseau: '[n]ature lays her commands on every animal, and the brute obeys her voice' (Rousseau 1973: 54). By contrast, '[m]an receives the same impulsion, but at the same time knows himself at liberty to acquiesce or resist: and it is particularly in his consciousness of this liberty that the spirituality of his soul is displayed' (Ibid.: 54). Echoing but also extending Rousseau, Marx maintains in 1844 not only that humans produce self-consciously rather than instinctively, but further, that 'man produces even when he is free from physical need and only truly produces in freedom therefrom' (Marx 1964: 113). Indeed, '[m]an therefore also forms things in accordance with the laws of beauty', says Marx (now invoking Kant) (Ibid.: 114). The fact that activity that could be, and should rightly be, one of art-making is turned into instrumental drudgery is the horrifying irony of alienation from species-being. The perversion of those powers the expression of which constitutes the *energeia* (or fully manifest being) of human beings, to use Aristotle's term, is a different order of harm than is the maldistribution of wealth or even the structure of ownership that both generates inequality and forecloses human flourishing.

No one disputes that in the *1844 Manuscripts* – wherein Marx is still talking about 'the negation of the negation' not being sufficient to usher in a fully realized collective subject – we find an account of how, in capitalism (called there 'estranged labour'), we have a spectacular example of humans having created a society in which our own creative powers function to dehumanize and to constrain us. It is less standard to look to *Capital* for an argument to this same effect. But we can and should do so (cf. Groff 2015). At the end of Chapter 4 of volume 1 of *Capital*, on 'The General Formula for Capital', Marx declares, '[b]ut now, in the circulation of M-C-M^1, value suddenly presents itself as a self-moving substance which passes through a process of its own, and for which commodities and money are both mere forms' (Marx 1976: 256). What is this 'self-moving substance'? What Marx himself wants us to know is that self-valorizing value, as he also calls it, is value that has become capital. 'M-C-M^1', he declares at the end of the chapter, 'is therefore the general formula for capital, in the form in which it appears directly in the sphere of circulation' (Ibid.: 257). Now, we are accustomed to thinking of capital as dead labour. In this regard, M-C-M^1 represents one valorization cycle, one 'social metabolic' process of successfully turning a given quantity of value in the form of money into a larger amount of value in the form of money. The increase is achieved, says Marx, via the purchase and use of the one commodity that can produce value, namely: labour power. M goes to M^1 because workers produce more value (in the commodity form; the product must be sold in order for the value in the product to be turned back into money) than is contained in the wage, provided only that the workday is long enough. The ΔM is nothing other than unpaid-for labour power: 'surplus value', as Marx calls it. With each valorization cycle, the value of this past (hence 'dead') unpaid-for labour figures into the outlay of value (in the form of money) deployed afresh as capital. But I want to say something more than that capital is dead labour. I want to say that value itself – 'this social substance', as Marx refers to it in chapter 1 – is the species-defining creative capacity of a society as a whole, when that society is a capitalist one – i.e. it is that collective human capacity when it is alienated in a specifically capitalist manner.

There are various reasons for thinking that value is alienated species-being. One is that the conditions that Marx treated as constitutive of estrangement in the *1844 Manuscripts* persist in what I shall call the *Capital* case. Three of the four we can track easily. Alienation from the *object* of labour, as per 1844: workers who have sold their labour power do not own or control the products of their labour (not unless they buy them, at which point they revert to being only use values). Alienation from the *process* of labour, as per 1844: workers who have sold their labour power do not control the process of labour (not even when labouring has been merely formally subsumed, as Marx puts it, into the valorization process). Alienation from *others*, as per 1844: manifestly, in the *Capital* case there is both inter- and intra-class conflict. This leaves only alienation from *species-being*, where species-being has been defined as our kind-specific capacity to engage freely with nature (which includes us) and to shape it (and ourselves) in our own image. Is this aspect of estrangement also carried forward into *Capital*? And if so, where do we find it? Yes. One place is at the start of Chapter 7 of volume 1. Here we find, in Marx's extended commentary upon the natural process of labouring as opposed to the production of surplus value, language akin to that of the description of species-being in the *Early Manuscripts*. Once again there is reference to 'the free play of [our] own physical and mental powers' and our abilities, as a species, to impose our will upon nature, as he puts it (for better or for worse) – which free play is contrasted with capitalist wage-labour (Marx 1976: 284–5). Even more striking, we are told that value just *is* a bizarre version of human efficacy, which is why labour power is the only source of it. More specifically, value – as I contend – is what distinctively human efficacy is *in the context of the very definite conditions of capitalist economic production*. Value is alienated species-being.

If this reading is correct, and alienation from species-being is just as central to *Capital* as it is to the *1844 Manuscripts*, then we can and should ask if there is (even) more to be learned from *Capital* about alienation than what can be learned from the early work – other, that is, than the meticulous outlining of (a) the mechanisms of surplus extraction via the wage relation and (b) the immiserating dynamics of accumulation. I think that the answer is again 'Yes'. If nothing else, *Capital* contains the discussion of the fetishism of commodities in section 4 of chapter 1 of volume 1, which directs our attention to the phenomenon of reification in a way that the earlier treatment of alienation does not. In the fetishism section, Marx makes a number of key points about alienation. In its most immediate and narrow sense, the depiction of capitalist commodities as fetishes is meant to underscore the fact that we think that the exchange-value of commodities is grounded in, or indicative of, their natural properties, when in fact it is a function of how much labour power (generic, abstract and averaged across a sector or society) went into their production. In Aristotelian terms, it is as though the artisan-imposed forms of artefacts were thought to be given by the artefacts' material causes – or, to put it more succinctly, as though artefacts were thought to be substances. This is a sharper and more technical account of the making-strange of the human capacity to shape nature than that which we find in 1844, and it also tells us something qualitatively new. The claim here is that the capacity in question has been *projected onto* those very objects that, as per 1844, workers produce but do not own or control.

More broadly, the notion of the fetishism of commodities conveys the thesis that, in capitalism, the 'world of commodities', as Marx puts it, has become a repository for the sociality of the whole society, not just for the (alienated) efficacy of the working class. Here too, we have an account of estrangement – especially from others – that goes beyond that of 1844. In the early manuscripts, alienation from others refers only to the fact of class. This is the stuff of the dramatic flair of the close of Part 1 of volume 1 of *Capital*, namely: 'He who was previously the money-owner now strides out in front as a capitalist; the possessor of labour-power fallows as his worker. The one smirks self-importantly ... the other is timid and holds back, like someone who has brought his own hide to market' (Marx 1976: 280). But now we are being told about a whole society, the individual and collective agential capacities of the members of which have been projected onto the dynamics of capital accumulation – i.e. really have assumed the form of self-valorizing value, such that the fetishism involved is not just an illusion or mistaken belief. This is, if not a different story altogether, at least a much further-reaching, all-encompassing one than that of class alone. This latter story is what Marcuse is referencing when he talks about the social reason that prevails in a given social formation, in the quoted passage with which I began. The social reason that encompasses *technē*-in-capitalism is alienated social reason.

Technology and Flourishing

I want to frame this part of the discussion by reiterating that there is a structural similarity between Aristotle's account of human flourishing and the normative stance embedded in Marx's notion of alienated species-being (see Groff 2015). As Aristotle has it in the *Nicomachean Ethics* (Aristotle 1962), humans flourish when we excellently actualize our characteristic rational powers in, or as, one and/or the other of two activities: contemplation and/or politics. The former involves the display of *sophia* (*nous* plus *epistēmē*); the latter the display of *phronesis*. The exercise of the power of *technē*, by contrast, for example in farming or mechanics, does *not*, in Aristotle's view, amount to a fully lived, fully flourishing (Greek, male) human life. Indeed, carpenters and mechanics, Aristotle tells us in Book 7 of the *Politics*, should not even be counted as citizens in an ideal *polis*. Their work is a necessary 'condition', of an ideal or proper *polis*, as he puts it, but they are not to be thought of (or treated as) 'parts' of that same *polis* (Aristotle 1995: 1328a21–1328b2).

The foregoing is obviously not Marx's vision. But Marx does claim for us a species-specific kind essence – a 'species-being' – the realization of which (historical, now, post-Hegel) is – as I read Marx – the good for human beings. I do not want to be misunderstood here. To be sure, Marx's conception of our essence is not Aristotle's. For Marx, it is precisely our power to shape nature that is essential: humans alone have the ability to produce according to the laws of beauty; in this sense, it is the rational power of *technē* that is at the heart of Marx's conception of flourishing. Moreover, Marx's *technē* is not Aristotle's. Marx includes humans in the category of nature in a way that (even) Aristotle does not. I alluded to this point previously. Marx's *technē* is therefore not only a power to impose new forms upon substances or even to turn artefacts into other artefacts. It is also a power to transform ourselves and our relationships with one another: in other words, to make our own history – to be self-determining. In this latter sense, the phenomenon of *technē*, in Marx's thought, coincides – in keeping with a Kantian inflection of the phrase 'the laws of beauty' – with that of freedom, conceived in terms of the metaphysically spontaneous self-conscious display of our creative faculties. Finally, having designated a wider, more integrated array of human powers as essential than did Aristotle, Marx's vision of flourishing differs from Aristotle's accordingly. Instead of a *polis* governed by wise members of the owning class, united by bonds of civic friendship, Marx imagines as a proper realization of our species-being a classless society, collectively self-governed, without need for the institution of the state. Despite these differences, however, the normative infrastructure of the view is recognizably Aristotelian: to flourish as a human is to exist fully as the kind of thing that humans (potentially) can be.

The question, then, is what use can we make of all of this when it comes to thinking about technology proper, and perhaps about automation in particular? Here again, let me start with Marx himself, who devoted 147 pages to the topic of automation in Chapter 15 of *Capital,* volume 1, 'Machinery and Large-Scale Industry'. Marx begins by distinguishing between what he calls 'manufacture' and what he calls 'large-scale industry', respectively. 'In manufacture', he writes, 'the transformation of the mode of production take labour-power as the starting point' (Marx 1976: 492). By contrast, '[i]n large scale industry ... the instruments of labor are the starting-point' (Ibid.: 492). Manufacture involves what Marx calls 'tools', rather than 'machinery'. Machinery and tools are alike in that (to quote Marx at length): 'like every other instrument of labour, machinery is intended to cheapen commodities and, by shortening the part of the working day in which the worker works for himself, to lengthen the other part, the part he gives to a capitalist for nothing. The machine is a means for producing surplus value' (Ibid.: 492). Machinery and tools differ, however, in that machinery, unlike 'an implement used in a handicraft' (Ibid.: 492), reduces workers to mere 'motive power[s]' thereof (Ibid.: 497). Tools are used, by workers, to make artefacts. Machines also require a 'prime mover' (Marx, using Aristotle's language), but (a) it is 'purely accidental' that it be a human being ('wind, water or steam would just as well take a man's place', Marx notes) (Ibid.: 497); and (b) as a rule, machinery increasingly 'requires a more massive mechanism [than humans] to drive it' (Ibid.: 497). Once machinery has reached a sufficient level of development, it is even further removed from any active role played by human beings. At this stage, when machinery itself comes to operate other machines, it constitutes what Marx calls an 'extensive apparatus' (Ibid.: 499). Next comes not just 'the cooperation of a number of machines of one kind', but 'a complex system of machinery' (Ibid.: 499), amounting to a kind of technological analogue of what Marx calls in the previous chapter the 'collective worker', namely, an integrated totality of machines, possibly set in motion themselves by 'an automatic centre' (Ibid.: 503).

Marx spends the rest of the chapter on machinery detailing the effects on production of automation at this scale, including changes in the rate of exploitation, the value of products, the level of the wage, and the social composition of the workforce. In other words, we are shown – as per the *Manifesto* – how the forces of production influence the relations of production. For present purposes, it is enough to observe that Marx is clear not only that, in capitalism, 'the machine is a means for increasing surplus value' (Ibid.: 492, cited above) rather than being a means to enable workers to engage in life activities other than labour, but also that, with the advent of large-scale, fully automated industry, workers are maximally alienated from the process of labour, as well as from other workers and from owners alike. In short, automation, in the context of estranged labour, necessarily increases alienation in all four of the senses of the term set out in the early manuscripts. 'This is the negative side' of automation, Marx says (Ibid.: 618). But there is a positive side too, according to Marx. Large-scale industry, Marx maintains, sets the stage for a transformation of 'the partially developed individual, who is merely the bearer of one specialized social function ... [into] the totally developed individual, for whom the different social functions are different modes of activity he takes up in turn' (Ibid.: 618). The minimal requirements of the Factory Act in particular, he observes, are a harbinger of the comprehensive technological education that he expects will be a feature of a post-capitalist division of labour, the ground for which is – or was, as Marx had it, at the time that he was writing – being laid by the dynamics of the present one.

In sum, then, Marx tells us that automation, in the context of capitalist production – i.e. capitalist automation – is contradictory. On the one hand, it brings with it maximal degradation of workers, including the women and children whom it necessarily pulls into the labour market (at least in the absence of regulation). On the other hand, it sets the stage for an entirely new mode of production, one characterized by a blossoming of capacities even at the level of the individual, and even just with respect to the individual's life as a worker. One part of the positive forecast has a familiar Aristotelian ring about it, albeit an Aristotle once again run through Hegel, with its projected realization of kind-specific potential (Aristotle), achieved historically and cast in terms of universality (Hegel). Another part of it is often read as Kantian: we will escape the sphere of necessity that is imposed upon us by nature and enlarged by the demands of the Law of Value, by having machines do most of the non-capitalist work. Note, though, that even this Kantian-toned facet of the vision is consistent with Aristotle's observation that labouring takes time. More important, remember too that, as Marx has it, human labouring is not necessarily onerous. Exactly to the contrary, it can – though it does not in capitalism – uniquely involve the freedom that Kant associates not with escaping the phenomenal realm for the noumenal, but rather with the spontaneity of aesthetic judgement.

So where does all of this leave us? I think that what we can take from Marx are some helpful guidelines for how to parse issues related to the use of technology, rather than a hard and fast answer to the question of whether or not to do so, and if so when. First, Marcuse – who learned it from Marx – is right to remind us that technology is always the technology of a given mode of production. The point here is not simply that certain types of tools and/or machines *accompany* given modes of production, though it is the case that they do. Rather, as Patrick Murray and Jeanne Schuler bring out beautifully in *Philosophical and Political Consequences of the Critique of Political Economy* (Murray and Schuler 2023; see also Engelskirchen 2011), a mode of production is the very form of social life at a moment in history, leaving its imprint upon the activities carried out in that time and place. Just as all concrete labouring bears the mark of the social relations in the context of which it is carried out, so too with technology. But the fact that a piece of technology has been produced as a capitalist commodity – and/or is part and parcel of the functioning of large-scale industry, say – does not settle the question of how that given piece of technology relates to human flourishing. Consider a Continuous Glucose Meter (CGM), which allows Type 1 and Type 2 diabetics to track their blood sugar levels in real time, and which notifies them (and any caretakers) of dangerous lows or highs. As what Marx calls 'use-vales', CGMs are lifesaving, regardless of their existence as, and role *qua*, a quantity of value in the commodity form. Moreover, in this example, for instance, the CGM promotes flourishing even if (in addition to the technology having a value-form) the increased incidence of Type 2 diabetes is itself at least in part a by-product of capitalism. And having come this far, we must engage now in dialectics. The air-conditioning that, because of capitalism, has become necessary to sustain human life in many regions of the world, and which is therefore patently life-enhancing in the short term, accelerates the very climate change from the effects of which it provides shelter. All while air-conditioners, from the perspective of capital, are just quantities of value, subject in their construction, production and operation to the demands of valorization. With respect to Marcuse's observation that technology is always fused to a given mode of production, an important upshot is that what that mode of production is, is not enough to determine whether or not any particular piece of technology that is fused to it contributes to human flourishing. The mode of production may be antithetical to flourishing – may be killing the planet, even, as capitalism is – while a particular technological item that is intertwined with it may make life demonstrably better, or even possible at all.

If it is not decided by the mode of production to which it is wed, is there some other test that might help us to evaluate a given piece of technology? I will offer a tentative yes. Of primary concern, it seems to me, is how a technology stands vis-à-vis the realization of species-being. Immediately we can see that a particular danger posed by automation is that of increased reification via machines taking on the activities of humans. A crucial variable in the case of automation, therefore, will be which activities have been handed over, and why. The human task taken on by a self-cleaning oven (namely, maintaining the inside of the stove) is one that we might not mind delegating to a machine. A computer program that obviates the need for humans to be able to compose musical scores or other works of art, or even a heartfelt letter of gratitude or apology, is a different matter. In the latter case, the 'tasks' that have been off-loaded onto a machine are ones the doing of which we might regard as integral to human flourishing. But there are dialectical twists even here. For example, from either an Aristotelian *or* a Marxist perspective, human flourishing includes a developed and actualized capacity for virtuous relationships with others. It follows that we might judge it bad to replace our friendships, to use Aristotle's vocabulary, with interactions with a chatbot. However, loneliness – itself exacerbated by capitalist social relations – is a health hazard, and one can see the appeal, and maybe even the worth, of automated companionship for those who are isolated. Thus, there may be a good to be had from chatbots depending upon the circumstances. Even so, we can ask about the quality of the simulated human-to-human relationship. To use Aristotle's typology from the *Ethics*: is it a utility-friendship, a pleasure-friendship or a character/virtue-friendship? John Symons and I have argued elsewhere that machines are not capable of *phronesis*. If we are correct, then a chatbot could never be an Aristotelian character/virtue-friend (Groff and Symons 2024). We may have good reason, then, to conclude that chatbots, while potentially helping to ameliorate the isolation that is endemic to capitalist society, at the same time undermine flourishing in that they are limited in how they can interact with us and therefore are limiting in how we are called upon to interact with them. In addition, they do indeed, by definition, take the place of a human interlocutor. But again, a young person without access to anyone kind in their human circle may survive into adulthood only thanks to a chatbot.

While it does not resolve dialectical contradictions, the diagnostic criterion that I have proposed – whether a given technology either contributes or detracts from the realization of species-being – is enough to allow for comparative assessments, at least. For instance, it seems to me that Zoom, for instance, carries less of a danger of reification (and/or of atrophy of relevant capacities) for one who is isolated than does reliance upon a chatbot, since in the Zoom case one is interacting with actual human beings. Though, again: the availability of technologically mediated ways to be in contact with far-flung friends and family might lessen the motivation to create local bonds, and it is unlikely that we would want to endorse the use of Zoom over in-person interactions where the latter are possible.

Similarly, spellcheck helps bad spellers know when they have misspelled a word without securing the services of a proofreader. There is a human cost to this, but we can see that it is smaller, less undermining of our kind-essential social and intellectual capacities alike, than that of having AI write whole texts for us.

Notice that the normative contradictions that I have been highlighting are less diachronic than those that Marx points to in *Capital*. As I read him, Marx is suggesting that capitalist technology is unreservedly bad in the present, but that it sets the stage for something unreservedly good. Even Marcuse is focused on the fact that the technology that is bad in one context might not be so in a different context. I have restricted my thinking to the capitalist present, suggesting that, in the present, capitalist technology can be both good and bad at the same time, relative to the kind-essential good for human beings.

Conclusion

By way of conclusion, let me just restate, this time without the dialectical complexities, what I think we can learn from Marx, when it comes to thinking about technology in general and automation in particular. First, via Marcuse, we are reminded that all technology has a social form, and that because the prevailing relations of production are capitalist, technology and capitalism are intertwined. There is no technology that is not, in the context of capitalism, capitalist technology. This is so whether we are talking about the role of automation in the workplace in the production of surplus value or the fact that technological devices are themselves capitalist commodities, i.e. quantities of value, including surplus value. Second, we find that we should be suspicious of any artefact or type of artefact that, regardless of the mode of production within which it is embedded, stands to supplant or upend the full actualization of our kind-specific capacities. Insofar as Marx treats the power of *technē* itself as integral to our species-being, special attention will need to be paid to the effects of technology upon *technē* itself – a *technē* already conceptualized more expansively than it was by Aristotle, such that it takes in our ability not only to make physical artefacts, but to make history (albeit not in conditions of our own choosing) as an ongoing creative, distinctively human act.

References

Aristotle (1962), *Nicomachean Ethics*, trans., with introduction and notes, M. Ostwald, Indianapolis, IN: The Bobbs-Merrill Co.
Aristotle (1995), *Politics*, trans. E. Barker; revised with introduction and notes by R. F. Stalley, Oxford: Oxford University Press.
Engelskirchen, H. (2011), *Capital as a Social Kind*, London and New York: Routledge.
Groff, R. (2015), 'On the Ethical Contours of Thin Aristotelian Marxism', in M. Thompson (ed.), *Constructing Marxist Ethics*, Leiden: Brill.
Groff, R. and Symons, J. (2024), 'Is AI Capable of Aristotelian Full Moral Virtue? The Rational Power of Phronesis, Machine Learning, and the Metaphysics of Regularity', in W. A. Bauer and A. Marmodoro (eds), *Artificial Dispositions: Investigating Ethical and Metaphysical Issues*, London: Bloomsbury.
Lawson, C. (2017), *Technology and Isolation*, Cambridge: Cambridge University Press.
Marcuse, H. (1968), *Negations*, Boston, MA: Beacon Press.
Marx, K. (1964), *The Economic and Philosophic Manuscripts of 1844*, trans. M. Milligan; ed. and intro. D. J. Struik, New York: International Publishers Co.
Marx, K. (1976), *Capital, A Critique of Political Economy*, vol. 1, trans. B. Fowkes; intro. E. Mandel, London: Penguin Books, in association with *New Left Review*.
Mill, J. S. (1951), *Utilitarianism, Liberty, and Representative Government*, New York: E.P Dutton.

Murray, P. and Schuler, J. (2023), *Philosophical and Political Consequences of the Critique of Political Economy: Recognizing Capital*, London: Palgrave Macmillan.

Ollmann, B. (1971), *Alienation: Marx's Conception of Man in Capitalist Society*, Cambridge: Cambridge University Press.

Rousseau, J-J. (1973), 'A Discourse on the Origin of Inequality', in *The Social Contract and Discourses*, trans. and intro. G. D. H. Cole; revised and augmented by J. H. Brumfitt and J. C. Hall, London: Everyman's Library.

Wendling, A. E. (2009), *Karl Marx on Technology and Alienation*, London: Palgrave Macmillan.

6

Artificial Intelligence, Alienation and the Existential Conditions of Human Flourishing

Jeff Noonan

On 1 November 2023, representatives from twenty-eight countries and the European Union met in England to attend an Artificial Intelligence (AI) Safety Summit organized by the UK government. The signatories to the 'Bletchley Declaration' agreed that while AI 'presents enormous global opportunities', left unregulated these emerging technologies pose significant risks to existing social structures and human interests (Bletchley Declaration 2023). The summit did not cover some of the more exotic concerns that have some researchers worried. For example, transhumanist philosopher Nick Bostrom has warned his more naive champions of cybernetic superintelligences that such an entity might not be motivated by any human sense of good and instead regard organic life forms as an unwelcome competitor for energy (Bostrom 2012). Other contemporary scientists have worried out loud about the threat that an AI system suddenly grown autonomous from its human creators could pose to the future of human life (Rose 2023). The summit examined more mundane concerns which lack science fiction potential but are more immediately threatening: AI's potentially maleficent effects on cyber security, biotechnology development and disinformation. 'There is potential for serious, even catastrophic harm, either deliberate or unintentional', the declaration asserted, 'stemming from the most significant capabilities of these AI models' (Bletchley Declaration 2023). When one adds to these political concerns the probable economic effects of widespread adoption of AI systems, there can be little doubt that AI has the potential to cause epochal problems for existing social structures, norms and the expectations and self-understanding of existing and future people.[1]

While most critical concern focuses on the social, political and economic dangers that unregulated development of AI systems poses, I want to shift the conversation to address what I regard as a more basic problem: the way in which alienation from the embodied nature of human intelligence and creative capacities frames the understanding of Artificial Intelligence as potentially superior to our evolved cognitive abilities. I do not doubt that the concerns voiced in the Bletchley Declaration are legitimate, and I cannot exclude *a priori* the possibility that a superintelligent computer system might one day emerge, but I do not think that these dangers are the most significant. The belief that *Artificial* Intelligence will become superior to human intelligence is the most significant danger because it is the underlying motivation that drives the research programme.[2] This belief assumes that 'intelligence' is equivalent to information processing capacity and speed. Since AI systems can process information faster than human beings, they are more intelligent, if this metric is sound. I will argue that it is not.

I will touch on technical questions of machine learning and Large Language Models of generative AI like the (in)famous ChatGPT, but my main concerns are existential and ethical. I will argue that the belief that AI systems are destined to exceed human intelligence is a function of an alienated understanding of our own embodied bio-social nature. The equation of quantitative processing power and speed with intelligence as such ignores the most salient feature of human intelligence: it is rooted in a needs-grounded and caring relationship with its natural and social environments. All sentient life forms are vulnerable; their intelligence has evolved in lock-step with the specific requirements of their survival. Human cognitive capacities are not reducible to survival instincts and include our powers to interpret our world as meaningful, beautiful, just and life-capacity enabling. Nevertheless, no matter how high our speculations and poetry soar above the earth, they presuppose the conscious desire on the part of people who produce them to continue living and thus constant connection with the earth and other people in institutionally mediated social environments.

Human intelligence, I will argue, cannot be understood on the model of disembodied processing power. If human intelligence is always bound up in interpretive, interested, affective and normatively saturated relations to the natural and social world, then it cannot be exceeded by systems that neither feel, nor yearn, nor interpret, nor care. The belief that some day machines will not only answer prompts but write poetry and explain to us the meaning of life stems from an alienated disposition towards our own bio-social nature.[3] This alienation is the deep cause of whatever other problems AI will cause, because this disposition is what drives the belief that AI is needed to solve human problems.

My argument will be developed in three sections. In the first, I will examine what I take to be the crucial difference between human embodied intelligence and machine learning. Understanding that difference has a deflationary effect on one's interpretation of the existing capacities of AI systems like ChatGPT. While their ability to *construct* coherent responses to prompts is impressive, they lack the felt, caring, interpretive relationship to the world required of genuinely *creative* subjects. In the second section I will explain why, despite the obvious differences between human embodied intelligence and AI systems, their champions believe that these systems will soon surpass human intelligence and open up new evolutionary pathways beyond the limitations of organic life forms. I will argue that these arguments presuppose a deep alienation from one's embodied being. Technotopian hopes for the emergence of cybernetic superintelligence are a paradoxical function of lament for the supposed feebleness of human capacities, which manifests itself as a desire for the emergence of a superintelligence that will overcome these limitations, *but in so doing, give rise to the most perfect possible form of human life-enjoyment*. In the third section I will attempt to undermine these hopes by arguing that the goods that technotopians hope to free from the limitations that shape the lives of embodied mortals in fact *depend* for their value on those very limitations. If true, my argument will prove that the hoped-for apotheosis of machine learners would be the *destruction* of human goods, all of which depend upon effort born of the uncertainties and vulnerabilities of human life.

Construction and Creativity

In order to understand the structure and implications of the alienation from embodied being that underlies the hoped for transcendence of human intelligence by computing systems, one must understand the fundamental difference between machine intelligence and human cognitive capacities. Fortunately, one does not need to understand at the highest technical level the way in which systems like ChatGPT work because the important point concerns what ChatGPT and other machine learning systems lack, rather than how they do what they do, that matters. Nevertheless, having a basic understanding of how they 'learn' and construct their responses to prompts will set in sharper relief the lack that concerns me. Thus, I will begin with a general explanation of how these systems function.

Contemporary AI systems like ChatGPT do more than simply execute routines. Instead, they are programmed to recursively improve their performance on the tasks for which they have been designed. The adjustments that they make to their performance are not programmed into them by human designers but are functions of their dynamic organization. Machine learning systems are typically composed of two layers of sensors that their designers call neurons. The system is capable of adjusting the values of the inputs such that it can improve its performance over time, analogous to the way in which humans evaluate their own performance and work out practical strategies to improve it. As Terence Deacon explains, 'neural net algorithms' work by employing 'sensors to assess whether a given task was accomplished or not. In the case of failure, it could modify the operation to more closely approach the target result next time' (Deacon 2013: 486). Over time, the system 'incrementally modifies connection strengths between nodes in a network with respect to success or failure criteria in "categorizing" inputs' (Ibid.: 486). The assumption underlying neural networks is that human intelligence is largely a function of the dynamics of neuronal firing: improved performance, whether human or machine, is a function of changed patterns of neural wiring.

ChatGPT operates in this recursive fashion, but its remarkable capabilities are the products of its ability to detect and then geometrically represent statistical patterns that it detects in the huge samples of text that it processes. By constructing a geometrical model of the probability of one word following another, the system is able to produce cogent answers to an unlimited number of prompts.[4] The more text it samples, the better its performance becomes.

> Imagine a neural network that has been programmed to predict the next word ... It will be pre-loaded with a gigantic number of possible words. But before it's trained, it won't yet have any experience in distinguishing among them ... Over time ... little adjustments coalesce into a geometric model of language that represents the relationships among words, conceptually. As a general rule, the more sentences it is fed, the more sophisticated its model becomes ... the better its predictions.
>
> (Anderson 2023: 10)

The question is: how far can this sort of machine learning progress under its own power?

Some researchers have argued that the latest version of ChatGPT has manifested emergent properties that emulate higher cognitive functions thus far found only in human beings. One recent paper has argued that the system has displayed capacities that indicate that it has developed a 'theory of mind' (Kosinski 2023). In cognitive psychology theory of mind refers to the human ability to attribute feelings and beliefs to other people – to recognize that they are sentient beings who adopt definite emotional and epistemic dispositions towards their environment. 'Humans do not merely respond to verbal clues', Kosinski argues, 'but also automatically track others' *unobservable* mental states, such as their knowledge, intentions, beliefs, and desires' (Ibid.: 1). The researchers designed a simple experiment to test whether or not ChatGPT could successfully predict the behaviour of a test subject who was acting on the basis of incomplete information. The details are unimportant for present purposes, but the results help us understand what AI researchers think about the nature of 'intelligence'. ChatGPT was able to successfully predict the beliefs of the subject with more or less the same success rate as human beings. Therefore, the researchers concluded, it is plausible to argue that ChatGPT had developed the capacity to attribute mental states to persons.

If that were true, then the standard critique of machine learning, that developed by John Searle in his famous 'Chinese room' argument, would be defeated (Searle 1980). Searle argued that we should think of Artificial Intelligence on analogy with a man in a room who follows instructions about how to translate Chinese into English. He knows no Chinese whatsoever, but merely mechanically follows the instructions given to him to successfully execute the operation. That might be true of the function of each individual neuron in the network, the researchers conclude, but the intelligence is not a substance inherent in the individual neurons, but a function of the operation of the network as a whole.

> Vast neural networks underlying connectionist AI are more akin to the human brain than to the if-this-then-that instructions followed by the person in the Chinese room ... Searle's argument ... remains useful, but it only applies at the level of individual neurons ... Such Chinese Room like neurons should not be credited with thoughts and understanding. However, the networks manifest emergent properties that are not present in the individual neurons and cannot be anticipated or deduced by studying individual neurons in isolation.
>
> (Kosinski 2023: 20)

While it would be wrong to argue that it is ontologically impossible for a neural net to manifest emergent properties (after all, life is an emergent property of complex arrangement of non-living elements), I think that there are good reasons to conclude that existing AI systems are not attaining levels of intelligence on par with, much less exceeding, human beings. In order to understand my conclusion, we must examine the crucial difference between Artificial Intelligence and human intelligence.

There is no doubt that machine learning is a tremendous achievement of mathematical logic and computer engineering. However, the human intelligence that has been invested in these systems is the product not of a few decades of dedicated research, but over 3 billion years of evolution. I am not reducing human intelligence to a survival function but arguing that the connection between intelligence and survival in a threatening environment gives human intelligence a uniquely affective dimension that not only distinguishes it fundamentally from existing AI systems, but adds a richness to human understanding that cannot be approximated in a non-living machine. In the experiment referred to above, the test subject looks for an object in the last place that they had seen it, but, unbeknownst to them, someone had moved it. ChatGPT could successfully predict that the test subject formed a false belief, but what it could not understand, because its predictions are not like human expectations, is that, in real life, the false belief would have been accompanied by emotions. The person would have felt disappointed, or confused, perhaps even frightened or forlorn. In human life, 'knowing that' is inseparable from having 'feelings about'. Knowing that a significant object has been misplaced will always be accompanied by feelings of concern, worry, frustration or sadness. Even if one does not care about the object, one might fear that one is becoming forgetful and, if one is of a certain age, that forgetfulness might be a sign of cognitive decline. These emotional dispositions are not extraneous to, but essentially characteristic of, *human* intelligence. One sign of the alienation between AI researchers and their own embodied intelligence is that they can often note this sort of difference between machine and human intelligence, but yet persist in using the machine's capacity as normative.[5]

ChatGPT proves that coherent linguistic constructions can be formed on the basis of syntactical information alone. However, meaning is not reducible either to syntax or to the abstract definition of words. Not only does meaning depend upon social context, social context depends upon the sorts of affective dispositions that living subjects adopt in different environments. If the words 'looking at', 'sunset' and 'peaceful' follow each other with enough regularity, ChatGPT could answer the prompt: 'How do you feel when you look at the sunset' with the answer 'peaceful'. Does it therefore know what it feels like to look at the sunset? Of course not, because it has never seen anything or felt anything. It does not feel the tension of working and worrying all day, and therefore cannot feel the sort of release that 'peaceful' refers to in an expression like: 'After a long, miserable day I finally felt peaceful as I watched the sun set crimson behind the bridge.' Unless one has had those experiences, one does not understand just how much meaning is packed into that sentence: work as drudgery, the difference between the place of work and home or places of repose and leisure, the feeling of tension draining from the body, the reflective state that quiescent feelings sometimes put us into, not to mention the memories that might arise. None of this content is available to the AI system.

One can only regard Artificial Intelligence as potentially superior to human intelligence if one excludes from one's definition of intelligence the affective dimension. In order to exclude the affective dimension, one must regard sentience and life as accidental features of intelligent agents. AI draws on functionalist philosophy of mind to do just that. Functionalism maintains that intelligence is indifferent to the material substratum that defines the intelligent agent. 'it makes no difference' to the functionalist, Daniel Dennett explains, 'whether a system is made of organic molecules or silicon, so long as it does the *same* job. Artificial hearts don't have to be made of organic tissue, and neither do artificial brains – at least in principle' (Dennett 1991: 31). *In principle*, neural nets can therefore be constructed of electronic sensors or nerve cells: what matters for intelligence is how they operate (function) and not the elements of which they are composed.

The argument might be true as far as signal processing goes, but it hardly suffices from an understanding of human intelligence, as critics of functionalism rooted in the pragmatist tradition have argued. W. Teed Rockwell has authored one of the most powerful of those critiques. His argument is salient for my purposes because he demonstrates that one cannot understand human intelligence outside affective and sensuous relations to a world that *matters* for the agent. As this normative and affective relationship cannot be simulated, and because it defines the true richness of human cognition, no Artificial Intelligence can surpass human intelligence if it lacks these irreducible dimensions of human thought.

Rockwell constructs his account against the belief that human intelligence is a function of neural organization alone. Against the conclusion of Hilary Putnam's famous 'brain in the vat' argument, Rockwell maintains that it would be impossible for a scientist – be they as mad and evil as one can imagine – to convincingly simulate the multi-textured richness of human sensuous and cognitive experience (Putnam 1965). Therefore, there is no possibility that we are just 'brains in vats', or computer simulations, or any other variant of Putnam's thought experiment. Only actual, evolved, living creatures *care* about their world. Caring is therefore essential to human cognition.

> We have no evidence whatever that what happens in the brain creates conscious experience all by itself. Consequently, it seems sensible to conclude that the supervenience base for all mental events, including subjective experience, includes not only brain activity, but lies in the whole body and in those parts of the environment with which the conscious organism maintains ... a relationship.
>
> (Rockwell 2007: 206)

These relationships are not only physical but include, for human beings, emotional and normative elements.

Rockwell draws on the work of William James to construct a holistic understanding of human consciousness and cognition as engaged, interested relationships with the natural and social world. Human beings are not essentially brains and brains are not essentially data processors. Human beings are social self-conscious organisms that *concern* themselves with their world. We need to understand the world in order to survive, but our understanding is integrated with our emotional dispositions. Our thinking about problems generates different feelings, is always undertaken for practical ends, and these ends, in turn, are justified according to different value systems. The affective and normative elements are not extraneous features of our mental activity from which neural operations can be abstracted and distilled down to their binary–logical essence. 'Before we begin inquiry, we experience a world of things that we care about, and these cares presuppose goals to be strived for and dangers ... to be avoided. These goals and purposes shape our experience by pointing beyond our bodies and brains' (Rockwell 2007: 87). Even the most hard-headed scientist is motivated by awe and wonder at the complexity and intricate harmonies of the physical universe; mathematicians refer without embarrassment to their discipline as the study of the 'poetry' of the universe.⁶ These self-descriptions are not simply metaphorical add-ons to the real business of quantitative modelling but explain the deeper motivations without which there would be no scientific inquiry.

Deacon elaborates upon the role that sentience plays not only as motivation but as the foundation of the value-structures within which human beings live, think and act. 'Feeling', he argues, 'is active, not passive, because of its incessant end-directed nature' (Deacon 2013: 487). We *feel* hungry and make something to eat: the heights of culinary creativity are not a function of an abstract ability to play with symbols but grow up out of our need for food and our capacity to imagine and invent new and pleasing ways of satisfying that need. We puzzle at an anomalous phenomenon in nature and formulate hypotheses and design research programmes that try to explain them. In general, that which we lack: sustenance, understanding, fulfilment, motivate us to create that which does not yet exist: lunch, a new scientific theory, poetry that mirrors our deepest fears and highest hopes. There would be no neural functioning with the desire to live, understand and enjoy. Deacon concludes, correctly, that while machines compute, 'without [conscious] representation, computation is just machine operation, and without human intentionality, machine operation is just physical change' (Ibid.: 496). Intentions, moreover, are formed within an affective matrix in which emotion plays an essential role. Emotion 'is the tension that separates self from not-self; the way things are from the way they could be; the very embodiment of the intrinsic incompletion of subjective experience that constitutes its perpetual becoming' (Ibid.: 512). One might well wonder at the technical complexity that underlies ChatGPT's capacity to construct its responses to prompts and be impressed with its ability to pass the LSAT (Law School Admission Test), but until such a time as it cares about what it is doing, it will not even have scratched the surface of the depths of human intelligence, for human intelligence unfolds from our sense of there always being something outside ourselves, beyond our grasp, that interests us, scares us, makes us curious and desirous.

When a plan goes awry or an expectation is unmet, human beings do not simply rewire their neural net by adjusting the values of sensory inputs: they feel disappointed and either abandon the project (as beyond their capabilities or not as worthwhile as initially thought), or they recommit themselves to the goal and work out different approaches to attaining it. The fact that we must abandon some approaches or devise novel strategies does not mean that human thought is inferior to machine intelligence. In the third section I will argue that the need to work through failure is definitive of all human life-activity, indispensable to human flourishing, and the reason why the powers of an imagined superintelligence which could simply think its goals into virtual reality would not be humanly satisfying. The human capacity to create and to experience the world as a source of both meaning and life is bound up with the frames of finitude within which we live: liability to disease and ageing, the possibility of failure, and death (see Noonan 2018: 4). I called these experiences 'frames' to emphasize that they do not determine the content of any human life but structure the experiential field within which any life must be lived. Unless we reflect upon and accept these frames (philosophically, or spiritually, or aesthetically, or scientifically, or some synthesis of all four ways of understanding), individuals will always be disappointed by the real limitations that characterize the scope and depth of capacity-development over the course of their lives and that ensure that some of our projects will fail. Only the species as a whole, developing over an open-ended future, could *fully* develop and realize *all* human capacities. The concrete development of life-capacities in concrete individuals is, in comparison, always partial and success uncertain. However, that even the richest life leaves innumerable projects unrealized and that some do not work out will not be a cause for dissatisfaction, *if* people interpret the quality of their lives within the frames of finitude which structure them. Outside those frames of finitude does not lie a better human *life* at all, but only a technotopian dream. Once we recognize the self-undermining implications of the dream of a human life without limitation, we can refuse existential despair at our condition and invest our energy in projects whose value is a function of the contribution to life that they make. The intensity of our efforts to realize them is a function of the fact that we might always fail. Since we live in a world that has its own dynamics and integrity, we must learn to work with and transform it. While our survival, development, flourishing and life-enjoyment depend on success, the meaning and value of success is shaped by the ever-present possibility of failure. As I will now explain, those who believe that the functioning of neural nets has the capacity to exceed human intelligence and solve the fundamental political, scientific and existential problems within which we struggle and live our lives have become deeply alienated from these frames of finitude and, therefore, human embodied being and intelligence.

Alienation from Species-Being for the Twenty-first Century

Marx's concept of alienation became a foundation stone for the critique of all forms of stultifying, one-dimensional social relations. The importance of the concept has been renewed in the recent work of Rahel Jaeggi, who wanted to revitalize the idea, extend its application to the critique of relationships beyond class and work life, and free it from what she regarded as the 'essentialism' that shaped Marx's understanding. In Jaeggi's view, Marx's critique of the alienating effects of capitalist social relations presupposed a concept of a 'true self' defined by objective needs and a fixed set of life-capacities. She argues that Marx's conception 'depends on ideas that are far from self-evident: from whom or what is one alienated ... By what standard do we recognize genuine needs ... what capacities do we have to develop in order to be whole human beings or a fully developed personality?' (Jaeggi 2014: 27). Jaeggi proposes to solve this purported problem by reconceiving alienation as a particular form of distorted relationship to the world and oneself (as opposed to the blocking of avenues by which one's 'true' self may be expressed).

While Jaeggi's efforts to widen the application of the category of alienation to experiences outside the capitalist workplace should be applauded, her critique of Marx's purported 'essentialism' detracts attention from the embodied basis of human experience, intellect and activity. Her definition of alienation as a 'relation of relationlessness' is less than clear and leaves the crucial question of who is related to what unanswered (Jaeggi 2014: 1). Hartmut Rosa, commenting on Jaeggi, tries to explain her paradoxical turn of phrase as referring to an experience in which 'our relationships no longer speak to us; they confront us as mute or even threatening' (Rosa 2019: 178). Jaeggi's original and Rosa's translation still leave the core problem unaddressed: if one is alienated, one must be alienated from something, and if one is alienated from some aspect of one's self (as in the case that interests me here), then that aspect of the self must be knowable, definable and distinguishable from a somehow damaged version of it. Unless human experience is structured by core needs and driven to unfold some fundamental life-capacities, one could not distinguish alienated from non-alienated practices and relationships.

I have examined the problem of the distinction between needs and consumer desire as well as the relationship between human flourishing and life-capacity realization in detail elsewhere (Noonan

2012). For present purposes, Jaeggi's worries can be allayed by turning to the criterion of need developed in the work of John McMurtry. While McMurtry also had concerns about the adequacy of Marx's understanding of needs, he remained committed to an objective distinction between needs as life requirements and consumer demands as subjective wants. Whereas in the case of genuine needs, deprivation of the resource or relationship in question leads to objective harm, in the case of consumer demands, their non-satisfaction not only is not objectively harmful, it may be beneficial by freeing the person's time from meaningless pursuits. McMurtry avoids the fruitless and impossible task of providing a complete list of fundamental needs and instead gives us a criterion by which needs claims can always be tested: 'N is a need, if and only if, and to the extent that, deprivation of n always results in a reduction of organic capability' (McMurtry 1998: 164). Need satisfaction is therefore an instrumental good. The intrinsic value of our lives is expressed through the development of our organic capacities for sentient awareness, cognition, communication, mutualistic relationship and creative activity.

Jaeggi is correct to worry about the implications of an abstract concept of a human essence, both because human beings change as their social practices change and because it has been historically deployed to justify pernicious distinctions between groups who purportedly meet the criteria of full humanity and those that do not. Nevertheless, one must guard against conflating an abstract and ahistorical conception of 'essential powers' from an historically grounded, materialist understanding of fundamental requirements of life whose particular content can change over time but whose functional contribution remains the same. One can satisfy nutritional requirements any number of symbolically mediated ways, but anyone who does not satisfy them will die. The same holds true with our capacities for experience, thought, creative practice and mutualistic relationship. Different people find different ways of life satisfying; one is not more 'essentially' human than another. There are innumerable ways to live a valuable life and all are good, provided only that one's own satisfactions are not predicated upon the systematic denial of others' access to the resources that they need to live their lives. Each social self-conscious human agent must reflect and decide how to develop their capacities in ways that are meaningful for themselves and make life-valuable contributions to their world. Better and worse lives are not distinguished by abstract and ahistorical measures derived from an idea of the human essence, but by examining historical struggles against systematic deprivation. Oppressed people live worse lives than their oppressors, precisely because they are prevented from freely exploring and realizing their life-capacities, but instead treated as mere objects to be used up and discarded. Whatever it is that people choose to do when they are free to choose how they will contribute their talents to the world forms a singular expression of the general human good. Abstractly universal conceptions of a human essence are empty, but any coherent conception of alienation requires a historically concrete conception of objective human needs and life-capacities.

The proponents of untrammelled AI development present a peculiar case of being alienated from these human capacities themselves. It is not that they find themselves straightjacketed by alienated working conditions, as workers were in Marx's view. On the contrary, they invest their intellectual capacities into the project of creating an Artificial Intelligence that will exceed their human powers, because they find their human capacities themselves inadequate when measured against what they imagine AI systems have the potential to become. An expanded interpretation of Marx's conception of alienation from species-being reveals much more clearly the depth problem than Jaeggi's idealist revision of the category. I will thus retain Marx's general understanding of alienation as a structure of experience in which the needs and capacities that distinguish human beings as a social self-conscious species appear as external, oppressive forces. However, in the case at issue here, alienation is more existential than social. The cause of technotopian alienation is not a function of particular social relationships that could be modified by political struggles. Their experience of alienation is a function of comparing what they are as embodied beings with what they imagine they could become by merging with evolving AI systems. Their solution to their alienation is techno-scientific development.

Jaeggi discusses Marx's conception of alienation from species-being but focuses only on the way in which capitalist social relations disrupt the ability of workers to realize the projects that they conceive freely (Jaeggi 2014: 14–15). Marx defines human species-being as our general capacity for 'conscious life-activity' (Marx 1975: 276). Unlike other species, human beings can imagine projects and realize them through practical–creative activity. Our imaginations are not tied down by immediate contexts; we can invent worlds and collectively work to make them objectively real. However, since labour is commodified under capitalism and employed only when and how it is profitable to do so, the world-creative power of labour is not freely developed but constrained and channelled by economic forces.

Marx thinks that the world-creative power of labour distinguishes human beings from other animals, but there is another, typically unremarked side of his conception of human beings that is more relevant to the diagnosis of technotopian alienation from our embodied being. Marx, still under the influence of Feuerbach in 1844, also focuses on the constraints within which human beings must labour to realize their ideas. He prefaces his comments about the freedom inherent in conscious activity with a discussion of our dependence on nature. Before we can freely create worlds, we must maintain ourselves in existence. As 'life-engendering life', labour must *respond* to a material world that conditions and constrains its activity (Marx 1975: 276). Our creative projects must take into account and serve the natural and social conditions of being alive. Once one focuses attention on those constraints, a certain tragic dimension to life inevitably opens up: that which it is possible for human beings to do is narrower than that which it is possible for them to conceive.

Marx argues that human beings are 'suffering beings', defined as much by what happens to them within the world as they are by what they can alter and create within the world (Marx 1975: 300). 'Suffering' is a function of the passive–receptive side of human beings. It does not refer to raw physical pain or mental anguish but to the fact that the world is external to us and functions according to its own dynamics. Experience is thus not a pure function of creating the world as we imagine it to be. Human beings must also undergo, that is, suffer, experiences of feeling needs and the limitations of our powers, whether we want to feel those pangs and constraints or not. We suffer because of the frames of finitude within which we live. Those frames are not functions of social conditions (although social conditions can modify their effects) but our embodied being. While they constrain our powers, they do not undermine their value, but help give them concrete form. Properly understood, Marx notes, our human limitations are 'a kind of self-enjoyment of man' (Marx 1975: 300). I will explain the connection between limitation and life-enjoyment in the final section.

AI proponents in general, and transhumanist technotopians in particular, find this gap between conceivability and material feasibility imposed by the frames of finitude unbearable. The alienation that underlies their research programme takes the form of an inability to understand the intrinsic connection between existence as a finite, embodied, bio-social subject and the experiences and activities that constitute the substance of the goods of human life. They interpret limitation as imperfection, and imagine that future AI systems, not subject to the limitations of organic intelligent beings, will prove superior, thereby creating the conditions for the solution of fundamental human problems and the limitless of enjoyment of the goods that we can only experience for finite amounts of time.

The purported benefits of superintelligence range from the mundane to the fantastical. Pattern recognition software, because it purportedly functions on the basis of pure data analysis, can, its promoters hope, generate human-bias free understanding of everything from earthquakes to crime waves (Bridle 2023: 140–2). Going one step further, Sam Altman of OpenAI believes that coming iterations of his company's creation will improve art and solve long-standing geopolitical problems. 'Everyone will have beautiful homes ... music will be enhanced ... Superhuman AI could help us to "treat each other better" and [solve] geopolitical problems [because] "We're so bad right now at identifying win–win compromises"' (Anderson 2023: 35). But even these hopes pale in comparison to the goals of the technotopian transhumanist wing of AI supporters. At the outer limits of speculation, Ray Kurzweil argues that once AI enters onto a self-ramifying evolutionary pathway it will undergo an apotheosis. 'In every monotheistic religion God is ... described as ... infinite knowledge, infinite intelligence, infinite beauty, infinite creativity, infinite love ... evolution moves inexorably toward this conception of God' (Kurzweil 2005: 389). Note that in each case these proponents of AI treats the experiences and practices that only human beings, with their defining needs and the tensions and conflicts that they generate, can understand, as problems that humans cannot solve, *because* we experience the needs and the tensions and the limitations. The solution to all these problems, in their view, is to transcend the needs, tensions and limitations *that shape human life*.

In other words, their solution is to search for a purely computational solution to 'problems' that are not functions of computation at all but the intentional strivings that define human social life. No human problem is a problem caused by slow information processing speeds. Crime is a function of the content of the law, which serves definite interests and marginalizes others. AI crime predictors do not escape bias, they replicate the biases embedded in the data that trains the system (Bridle 2023: 146–7). War and peace are not only functions of deep-seated economic and political structures but also are opposed conceptions of just social arrangements. No AI system can determine win–win compromises in international relations. A win–win compromise is not a point of arithmetic balance between interests but also a function of what the contending parties take to be just. Human beings act not only on a theory but also out of a sense of justice. They are willing to compromise only when this sense of justice is not offended. Lacking feelings and therefore incapable of factoring into its calculations this irreducible affective dimension, AI cannot help us solve our conflicts. As for becoming god-like: even if AI enters onto the evolutionary pathway that Kurzweil imagines, it would not be human forms of the good that it would free from the limitations of its embodied forms. If it experienced any goods at all, they would be goods proper to a radically different form of life.

Technotopians think that they are carrying forward the values of Enlightenment humanist philosophers (More 1995). While it was true that Enlightenment philosophers of history like Condorcet hoped that the advance of science would indefinitely prolong human life and help us overcome the scourges of war and material inequality, they could not imagine that these goals would be achieved at the price of eliminating the embodied basis of human experience, thought and enjoyment (Condorcet 2018: 100–1). The technotopian appropriation of the humanist traditions leaves out the other side: the inquiry into how to live well within the frames of finitude that define human life.

Living within these frames means thinking of the goods of medicine as therapeutic and preventative; the goods of politics as a struggle towards institutional forms rooted in mutual understanding, respect, need-governed access to goods and service, and equal ability to all-round development and life-enjoyment; and the goods of science as deepening our understanding of the universe of which we are an evolved part. For the technotopians, any development of understanding and power that stops short of total mastery – indeed, total absorption of the material by the virtual world, appears as an unbearable limitation. This inability to bear the limitations definitive of human life is the express sign of their alienation from their embodied being, because they are alienated from their own embodied existence.

Failure and Flourishing

The difference between the virtual and material world is that the material world resists the imposition of our ideas onto its structures. Virtual reality – at least the absolute virtual reality imagined by computer engineers like Hans Moravec – would take on whatever form the superintelligence that generates it imagined it to be (Moravec 1999: 167–8). While the transcendence of the gap between conception and execution appears to be the fulfilment of the goal of creating the conditions for all-round human development, expression, enjoyment and flourishing, in reality their value depends upon their being achievements, and their being achievements depends on the possibility of failure.

No one wins the Nobel Prize for Literature for a series of novels they merely imagined; the Nobel Prize for Physics is awarded to scientists who explain the material universe as it has evolved, not as they would like it to be in order to make it more amenable to successful explanation. The novelist and the physicist, and also the young person struggling to make friends in a new environment, new parents trying to work out the best way to care for their child, the political movements deliberating about the best strategy and tactics have in common the knowledge – even if it is only in the background – that they might fail. The stakes of failure can be high indeed: political miscalculation could invite reprisals from a more powerful enemy that costs lives; bad parenting can lead to a lifetime of psychological problems in the child, and one's novel might prove derivative pulp rather than a prize-winning triumph. But if the possibility of failure were removed, so too would the intensity of effort through which our talents – slow and meagre as they might be – are developed. Some develop those talents more highly and more comprehensively than others, but everyone *feels* the value of that which they do in the effort they know they need to expend in order to achieve their goal. There would be no life-value to our experiences, practices, relationships, theories and creations if they were not forged in the crucible of possible failure.

The same must be said about the relationship between mistakes and human creativity. Creative activity is not a programmed function that merely executes a routine to achieve a desired result. As I noted above, we create within and using the materials of a world with its own dynamics and structural integrity. Neither nature nor other people simply do our bidding. In order to achieve our goals, we have to experiment with methods which may or may not succeed. However, we might also end up achieving a goal that we did not intend to achieve, which turns out to be superior to the goal that we intended to realize. I call these unintended consequences of creative experimentation and effort 'productive mistakes'. Viewed in the light of the original goal, the achieved result is not what we desired and intended and can therefore be classified as a mistake. Unlike ordinary mistakes whose results we discard, productive mistakes lead to new insights, successful practices or relationships, or pleasing works of art.

Artistic practice is perhaps paradigmatic, since rarely is a satisfying work of art simply a function of following rules. The American painter Robert Motherwell explains the relationship between the mistake and artistic achievement clearly: 'I begin every painting by painting a series of mistakes. The painting comes out of the correction of the mistakes by feeling' (Motherwell 2007: 255). The mistakes are purely a function of the arbitrariness of any starting point for an abstract painting. At some point – and this claim holds true for any human endeavour – one must decide to act, to do one thing rather than another, and see what happens. What happens, in many cases, is not that which one expected or even hoped. The result is not only good, but would not have been achieved unless the mistake had been made. One makes a date with someone for lunch, gets delayed, the date leaves, but you end up having coffee with a stranger and fall in love. To reduce creativity and the formation of relationships to an automated but infallible routine would destroy the uncertainty from which all of our most worthwhile projects begin.

We thus make ourselves into the distinct individuals that we become through a series of projects which unfold within a field of possible failures and mistakes. One of the surest signs of an unjust society is that whole groups of people, because they are poor or belong to a demonized, oppressed identity, are simply forced into a way of life by material circumstances and never have the real opportunity to choose between different forms of life. Justice, in the most general sense, means getting what one deserves. Since all humans are born with latent potential to develop their intellect, their emotional dispositions, their capacities for playing and for making, and no one chooses the needs that must be satisfied if these latent capacities are to be developed one way rather than another, no one deserves to be deprived of that which they need just because they were born. No one chooses to be born and no one can control the circumstances of one's birth. Generic justice demands that societies use their resources to satisfy the needs of the citizens that older generations bring into being.

People are owed a share of the collective wealth that everyone helps produce. No one is owed success in whatever endeavour that they choose to pursue and if they were, the very idea of success, and the sense of satisfaction that accompanies it, would be ruined. Yet, in a sense, guaranteed success is the ultimate aim of the technotopian research agenda. As we saw in the second section, their alienation from embodied human being is expressed by their dissatisfaction with the temporal and perspectival confines of human intelligence. Human minds focus on *this* which entails that they cannot simultaneously focus on *that*. The embodied finitude of human life imposes the need to choose, ultimately irrevocably, between alternatives. No matter how comprehensive the scope of an individual life, it must leave some projects unexplored because the development of projects requires time, and our time runs out. However, in their demands for unlimited intelligence and creative power, the technotopians forget that individuation presupposes limitation.

Human flourishing does indeed involve the realization of our intellectual, affective and creative capacities. But human beings flourish as definite, concrete individuals. People's interests and talents vary; we are not locked into ego-centric silos and we can delight in the achievements of others, but our life is lived through our unique self-conscious engagement with the world. Individual self-development and enjoyment is a function of choice to pursue one thing and therefore to forgo an unlimited set of other things that we might have chosen to pursue but could not. The fact that devotion to one project prevents an individual from pursuing other projects is not proof that bio-social life is radically impoverished in comparison to a cybernetic superintelligence. It means that *human flourishing is social*: the good of one life is only a part of the good of the more comprehensive good of the human project distributed over time and across social space, shared between individuals, each of whom expresses one part of a dynamic, developing whole. Those who understand the social nature of the human good will not be motivated to incorporate all possible goods into their own consciousness (by uploading themselves into the Singularity) but work against the social, political and economic forces that reduce the lives of some people to the status of mere objects of power. We do not need a future AI system to discover 'win–win compromises'. The history of past political, social and economic struggles is proof enough that human beings can understand our own problems and devise institutional solutions to them. Solutions are impeded not by the limitations of the human intellect but by social powers opposed to using collectively produced wealth to enable the full and free realization of individual life-capacities. The irony of turning the historical struggle for human *freedom* over to AI systems that will program our future for us is so obvious it needs no further comment.

A world which had overcome the fundamental social impediments to all-round self-development would still be a world in which there were existential impediments to *absolute* self-development. Accepting the limitations that define the bio-social human being is part of self-understanding, and self-understanding is part of making only such demands on life as can be potentially realized. The technotopian demand that AI free us from the frames of finitude within which human action and experiences unfold proves only their total lack of self-understanding and their alienation from their embodied *human* being. Human beings flourish in propitious social conditions, but no matter how egalitarian and democratic the social conditions, individuals – so long as we remain human – will have to devote ourselves to one form of life and not another. Humanists are those who celebrate having to make these choices – tragic as they sometimes are – because they strive to comprehend the human good as it develops and unfolds over the open-ended future of the species.

Collectively, over that open-ended future, we develop all the potentialities that it is possible for us to develop. Individuals living within historical time and cultural space become specific people by choosing to devote themselves to one field of endeavour. The technotopian project demands that each individual experience everything that it is logically possible to experience. Success in such a project would destroy the very individuality which is the basis of the enjoyment that the technotopians want to free from the necessary limits of embodied life. At best, individuals would be fictions that the Singular superintelligence invented for the sake of amusing itself. However, since it would be omniscient, it would see through its own ruse.

Notes

1 One report from Goldman Sachs that was widely cited in the spring of 2023 warned that 18 per cent of existing jobs could soon be automated, costing the global economy 300 million jobs (Toh 2023). However, most mainstream economists believe that the current wave of automation will follow a similar pattern to earlier waves. Technology will disrupt existing employment patterns but will create at least as many new opportunities as it will destroy old ones (World Bank 2019). Outside the mainstream, technotopian thinkers argue that instead of struggling to maintain employment levels, workers need to struggle to capture the productivity benefits of automation and strive towards a jobless future (Bastani 2019). The technotopians would solve the problem of alienated labour by freeing human beings from the need to labour entirely. Elsewhere I have argued that the argument in favour of a post-work society underestimates the value of work in a meaningful human life (Noonan 2021). Here I want to focus on

the deeper existential values from which that earlier argument developed. Post-work is a specific example of the generic alienation from our embodied human being that I will examine here.

2 Political and economic anxieties have spawned a veritable industry of AI ethics whose function is to determine the best means of channelling AI development in benevolent directions. A critical examination of this literature by James Steinhoff concludes that AI ethics uncritically presupposes that the development of AI is good and inevitable and simply provides justification for whatever outcomes the science makes possible. Steinhoff concludes that 'AI ethics … is ethics washing … [and] also serves the economic exigencies of data-intensive capitalism' (Steinhoff 2023: 1).

3 Margaret Atwood, hoping to allay the fears of her fellow poets that ChatGPT would replace their evocative powers, asked ChatGPT to construct a poem about her summer home on Pelee Island, a small island in Lake Erie and the southernmost inhabited landmass in Canada. Here is a fragment of its construction: 'Through the digital window, the world looks on, / As PIBO's mission is daily drawn. / From this mud-rich base, to lands afar, / Spread the lessons of life, each under a star.' One does not have to have ever visited Pelee to recognize this verse as rubbish worth even less than the doggerel of amateur poets. Atwood concludes 'that a chatbot replacing Uncle Roger might very well happen, but, dear published author, it is not yet very likely to replace you' (Atwood 2023).

4 A visual explainer published in *The Guardian* provides a very useful graphic model of ChatGPT's operation (Clarke et al. 2023).

5 Another group of researchers performed an analogous test for theory of mind in ChatGPT and was more sceptical of the results (Trott et al. 2023). Regardless of how the results are interpreted, the important point is that this group did distinguish the way in which ChatGPT approached the assigned task and the 'rich social and multimodal context' in which human beings form beliefs about how others are feeling or what they are thinking (Trott et al. 2023: 15). While they did not regard this difference as an insuperable barrier to the eventual emergence of novel, human-like capacities in ChatGPT, the fact that they mentioned the difference illustrates my point: the human intelligence is integrally cognitive–affective. Until AI is alive, it will not display human level intelligence because it will always lack the affective dimension.

6 I borrow the phrase from a book that I read years ago, *The Poetry of the Universe: A Mathematical Exploration of the Cosmos*, by the mathematician Robert Osserman. He borrowed the phrase from Einstein, whom Osserman quotes in the epigraph to the body of the text: 'Pure mathematics is, in its way, the poetry of logical ideas' (Osserman 1995).

References

Anderson, R. (2023), 'Does Sam Altman Know What He's Creating?' *The Atlantic*. https://www.theatlantic.com/magazine/archive/2023/09/sam-altman-openai-chatgpt-gpt-4/674764/ (accessed 22 November 2023).

Atwood, M. (2023), 'Margaret Atwood Reviews a "Margaret Atwood" Story by AI. https://thewalrus.ca/margaret-atwood-ai/ (accessed 11 December 2023).

Bletchley Declaration. (2023), *The Bletchley Declaration by Countries Attending the AI Safety Summit, 1–2 November 2023*. https://www.gov.uk/government/publications/ai-safety-summit-2023-the-bletchley-declaration/the-bletchley-declaration-by-countries-attending-the-ai-safety-summit-1-2-november-2023 (accessed 18 November 2023).

Bostrom, N. (2012), 'The Superintelligent Will: Motivation and Instrumental Rationality in Advanced Artificial Agents'. https://nickbostrom.com/superintelligentwill.pdf (accessed 8 December 2023).

Bridle, J. (2023), *New Dark Age: Technology and the End of the Future*, London: Verso.

Clarke, S., Milmo, D. and Blight, G. (2023), 'How AI Chatbots Like ChatGPT or Bard Work – Visual Explainer', *The Guardian*. https://www.theguardian.com/technology/ng-interactive/2023/nov/01/how-ai-chatbots-like-chatgpt-or-bard-work-visual-explainer (accessed 18 December 2023).

Condorcet, N. (2018), *Sketch for an Historical Picture of the Advances of the Human Mind*. https://www.earlymoderntexts.com/assets/pdfs/condorcet1795_3.pdf (accessed 15 December 2023).

Deacon, T. (2013), *Incomplete Nature: How Mind Emerged From Matter*, New York: W. Marx, K. ([1859] 1904), *A Contribution to the Critique of Political Economy*, Chicago: Charles H. Kerr & Company. W. Norton.

Dennett, D. (1991), *Consciousness Explained*, Boston, MA: Little, Brown and Company.

Jaeggi, R. (2014), *Alienation*, New York: Columbia University Press.

Kosinski, M. (2023), 'Theory of Mind Might Have Spontaneously Emerged in Large Language Models'. Arxiv.org https://arxiv.org/ftp/arxiv/papers/2302/2302.02083.pdf 1–31 (accessed 22 November 2023).

Kurzweil, R. (2005), *The Singularity Is Near*, New York: Penguin.

Marx, K. (1975), 'Economic and Philosophical Manuscripts of 1844', *Karl Marx and Friedrich Engels: Collected Works*, vol. 3, New York: International Publishers.

McMurtry, J. (1998), *Unequal Freedoms: The Global Market as an Ethical System*, Toronto: Garamond.

Moravec, H. (1999), *Robot: Mere Machine to Transcendent Mind*, Oxford: Oxford University Press.

More, M. (1995), *The Extropian Principles*. https://www.alamut.com/subj/ideologies/manifestos/extropian_principles.html (accessed 15 December 2023).

Motherwell, R. (2007), 'On the Humanism of Abstraction: The Artist Speaks, 1970', in D. Ashton and J. Benach (eds), *The Writings of Robert Motherwell*, Berkeley, CA: University of California Press.

Noonan, J. (2012), *Materialist Ethics and Life-Value*, Montreal: McGill-Queens University Press.

Noonan, J. (2018), *Embodiment and the Meaning of Life*, Montreal: McGill-Queen's University Press.

Noonan, J. (2021), 'Marxist Transhumanism?' *New Proposals: Journal of Marxism and Interdisciplinary Inquiry*, 12 (1): 63–75.

Osserman, R. (1995), *The Poetry of the Universe: A Mathematical Exploration of the Cosmos*, New York: Anchor Books.

Putnam, H. (1965), 'Brains and Behavior', in R. J. Butler (ed.), *Analytic Philosophy*, 1–19, Oxford: Oxford University Press.

Rockwell, W. T. (2007), *Neither Brain nor Ghost*, Cambridge, MA: MIT Press.

Rosa, H. (2019), *Resonance: A Sociology of Our Relationship to the World*, Cambridge: Polity Press.

Rose, S. (2023), 'Five Ways AI Might Destroy the World', *The Guardian*, 7 July 2023. https://www.theguardian.com/technology/2023/jul/07/five-ways-ai-might-destroy-the-world-everyone-on-earth-could-fall-over-dead-in-the-same-second (accessed 22 October 2023).

Searle, J. (1980), 'Minds, Brains, and Programs', *Behavioral and Brain Sciences*, 3 (3): 417–57.

Steinhoff, J. (2023), 'AI Ethics as Subordinated Innovation Network', *AI and Society*, Open Forum, 30 March 2023. https://doi.org/10.1007/s00146-023-01658-5 (accessed 15 December 2023).

Toh, M. (2023), '300 Million Jobs Could be Affected by Latest Wave of AI, Says Goldman Sachs'. cnn.com https://www.cnn.com/2023/03/29/tech/chatgpt-ai-automation-jobs-impact-intl-hnk/index.html (accessed 18 November 2023).

Trott, S., Jones, C., Chang, T., Michaelov, J. and Bergen, B. (2023), 'Do Large Language Models Know What Humans Know?' *Cognitive Science*, 47: 1–21.

World Bank (2019), *The Changing Nature of Work: World Development Report 2019*. https://documents1.worldbank.org/curated/en/816281518818814423/2019-WDR-Report.pdf (accessed 18 November 2023).

7

Marxism and the Idea of a Fully Automated Machine Society

Science Fiction Utopia or Dystopian Nightmare?

Tony Burns

There has been quite a lot of discussion recently about the social and political implications of automation for contemporary society (Benanav 2020; Danaher 2019; Skidelsky and Craig 2020; Susskind 2021; West 2018). Some of this literature has discussed the relevance of Marx and Marxism for any attempt to understand the significance of these developments (Fisher and Fuchs 2015; Frey 2020; Fuchs and Mosco 2015; Kassem 2024; Wendling 2009). However, the current and ongoing debate about the benefit or harm to the well-being of humanity as a whole that is brought about by the introduction of new technology and the historical development in the direction of a fully automated machine society is far from being a novelty.

With the development of AI and computing technology more generally, the specific character of the vision of a fully automated machine society in the future has changed significantly since Marx speculated about it in the nineteenth century. As W. H. G. Armytage has noted, in *Yesterday's Tomorrows: An Historical Survey of Future Societies*, the idea of what such a future society will be like has a history (Armytage 1968). However, although that is true, the idea of such a society and the debate about its consequences for the human condition pre-date the current controversy surrounding AI and have remained a perennial feature from the nineteenth century onwards. It is, for example, central to Karl Marx's theory of alienation, as set out in both the *Economic and Philosophical Manuscripts of 1844* and in the chapter on machinery in *Capital*, volume 1 (Marx [1844] 1967; Marx [1867] 1974).

The focus of this chapter is not so much on works of social theory or philosophy, but on works of literature, specifically works of dystopian fiction. The dangers associated with the emergence of a fully automated machine society in the future have been a staple topic for discussion by creative writers, especially the authors of works of dystopian science fiction, from its inception, whether one associates this with Mary Shelley's *Frankenstein* or the short stories of H. G. Wells at the end of the nineteenth century. One justification for this, if it requires one, is that creative writers are arguably better placed than philosophers and social theorists to communicate to their readers the dehumanizing consequences of living in a society that is becoming increasingly dominated by machinery. Moreover, the authors of the great works of dystopian fiction were all theoretically sophisticated individuals, who were familiar with the latest developments in science and technology in their own societies and times. They were as much engaged with social commentary as they were with producing works of art. This is evident if one takes into account their essays and journalism as well as the novels which made them famous. There is a distinct aesthetic dimension to the critique of technocratic utopianism and the idea of a machine society that has been offered by social theorists and philosophers (Marx [1844] 1967: 71–2; Marcuse 1978). It is arguable that those who are best placed to appreciate and communicate the full significance of this to their readers are artists generally and creative writers in particular.

In what follows I shall consider the views of the authors of three classical works of dystopian science fiction in the first half of the twentieth century, namely Yevgeny Zamyatin's *We* ([1920] 1972); Aldous Huxley's *Brave New World* ([1946] 1979); and George Orwell's *Nineteen Eighty-Four* ([1948] 1968). I shall focus mainly on the work of George Orwell, whilst also referring, as Orwell does at times, to the views of Zamyatin and Huxley. In the opinion of all three of these authors the idea of a fully automated machine society in the future is a bad thing. Such a society is something to be avoided and not pursued. Far from being a utopia, were it to come into existence it would be a dystopian nightmare (Amis 2000; Hillegas 1967; Walsh 1962).

One interesting feature of this dystopian literature is that all three of these authors associate this alleged nightmare vision of the society of the future with Marxism. They occasionally give their readers the impression that they are critics of Marxism as well as of utopianism. Their objection to the idea of the emergence of a fully automated machine society is a core component of their critique of Marxism, as they understand it. There are a number of different aspects to this critique, of which two in particular stand out. The first is their assumption that, according to Marxists, the communist utopia [*sic*] of the future will be hedonistic. The second is their assumption that decision-making in that society will be made by scientists, technicians and engineers, that is to say, by experts. In short, that society will be a technocratic scientific utopia. I will focus on the second of these issues.

So far as Marxism is concerned, I have discussed the views of Marx himself in two earlier contributions to the Automation Project (Burns 2023; Burns 2024). As I point out in these contributions, for Marx automation and the introduction of machinery into the production process are essentially the same thing. Marx had quite a lot to say on the historically progressive move in the direction of a fully automated machine society in his writings, including the chapter on alienation in the *Paris Manuscripts* of 1884 (Marx [1967] 1984), the 'Fragment on Machines' in the *Grundrisse* manuscript (1857–8) (Marx [1857–8] 1973), and the chapter on 'Machinery and Modern Industry' in *Capital*, volume 1 (1867) (Marx [1867] 1974). My focus in what follows will not therefore be on the ideas of Marx himself. Rather, it will be on how this issue was dealt with in the history of Marxism after Marx's death in 1883, especially by Marxists in Russia.

The chapter has two parts. In Part One I consider what Zamyatin, Huxley and Orwell have to say about the idea of a fully automated machine society, their reasons for thinking that it would be a bad thing. Here my main focus will be on the writings of Orwell, including his essays, journalism and correspondence, as well as his novel *Nineteen Eighty-Four*. In Part Two I discuss the debate around the idea of a fully automated machine society which took place between Marxists in Russia at the turn of the nineteenth and twentieth centuries. I argue that although the dystopian critique of Marxism that is offered by Orwell and his predecessors does have an application to the views of some Marxists in Russia, especially to those of Lenin, it does not apply to others. In particular, it does not apply to Alexander Bogdanov, one of Lenin's main Bolshevik opponents at this time. I suggest that, so far as their respective visions of the communist society of the future are concerned, it was Bogdanov and not Lenin whose views came closest to those of Marx himself. The two parts of the chapter are connected. The mediating link between them is the influence of H. G. Wells's technocratic vision of future society and the influence which it had on the authors of the great works of dystopian science fiction as well as on Marxists in Russia.

Part One: Dystopian Science Fiction and the Idea of a Machine Society

Tom Moylan's *Scraps of the Untainted Sky: Science Fiction, Utopia, Dystopia* provides what is arguably the best introduction to the history of dystopian science fiction (Moylan [2000] 2018). According to Moylan, one of the principal concerns of the authors of such works is the emergence of a machine society, a society in which not just working life but life in general has become dominated by machines. Moylan identifies E. M. Forster's *The Machine Stops* (1909) as the most significant precursor of this trend at the beginning of the twentieth century (Moylan [2000] 2018: 111–45). According to the authors of literary dystopias referred to earlier, this development is for a variety of reasons regarded as a bad thing. It is something to be avoided. The works in question are offered as a warning or a prophecy, the purpose of which is to contribute towards the effort to avoid the emergence of such a society.

George Orwell provides a very good illustration of what Moylan has in mind. Like Marx, Orwell was interested in the process of historical development on a world or global scale from a pre-industrial to an industrial society or civilization. The underlying tendency of history, he says, is in the direction of 'industrialism'. He associates this process with the introduction of new technology or machinery, and with 'machine production'. In *The Road to Wigan Pier* (1937), Orwell argued that humanity is moving increasingly in the direction of a 'machine society' (Orwell [1937] 1971: 164).

Although socialism, Marxism, communism in general, and Soviet communism in particular, are different (if related) things, Orwell tends at times to overlook the differences between them. In *The Road to Wigan Pier* he associates 'Socialism', in both Western Europe and the Soviet Union, and in theory as well as practice, with an unquestioned emphasis on the value of science and technology, and on the economic development which technological innovation can bring about. In Orwell's words, 'Socialism as a world-system implies machine-production'. Orwell argues that 'any world in which socialism was a reality would be at least as highly mechanized as the United States at this moment, probably much more so'. On this view, the socialist world is pictured as 'a completely mechanized, immensely organized world, depending on the machine as the civilizations of antiquity depend on the slave' (Orwell [1937] 1971: 165). In that world, 'all the work that is now done by hand' will 'then be done by machinery' (Ibid.: 166).

Orwell observes that this pro-machinery attitude of mind among socialists, in both the capitalist West and the communist [*sic*] East, is associated with the notion of progress and with modernization. Socialism, as usually presented, is he says generally 'bound up with the idea of mechanical progress, not merely as a necessary development but as an end in itself'. In the case of the Soviet Union, he claims, 'this idea is implicit' in 'most of the propagandist stuff that is written about the rapid mechanical advance in Soviet Russia (the Dnieper dam, tractors, etc, etc)' (Orwell [1937] 1971: 165). Orwell evidently agreed with Aldous Huxley's assessment of the Bolshevik view of communism as a mechanized 'utopia'. In an essay entitled 'The New Romanticism', published in 1931, Huxley states that 'to the Bolshevik idealist [sic], Utopia is indistinguishable from one of Mr. Henry Ford's factories'. He maintains that 'the communist State' in Russia 'requires, not men, but cogs in the huge "collective mechanism"', and that the 'condition of entry' into 'the Bolsheviks' Earthy Paradise' in Russia is that 'they shall have become like machines' (Huxley [1931] 1938: 214).

In *The Road to Wigan Pier*, Orwell draws attention to the existence of 'the kind of person', and indeed the kind of socialist, in East or West, 'who views mechanical progress, as such' (or for its own sake) 'with enthusiasm' (Orwell 1937] 1971: 165). He associates the mentality of such a person with the notion of 'machine worship'. This attitude, in 'its most completely vulgar, ignorant, and half-baked form', is, he argues, 'the authentic voice of a large section of the modern world', both capitalist and communist (Ibid.: 168). Orwell associates machine worship with a certain form of technocratic utopianism, of which he disapproved. Those who think in this completely uncritical way about the benefits of science and technology, he suggests, seem 'unable to grasp that the opposite opinion exists'. Hence they are blind to the existence of the drawbacks or the possible and indeed actual 'downside' of scientific progress, technological development and 'the present mechanization of the world' (Ibid.: 166).

Like Aldous Huxley in *Brave New World*, one of Orwell's targets is what he considered to be the naive and over-optimistic scientific utopianism of H. G. Wells, not the earlier Wells of the 1890s, who was author of the dystopian science fiction stories which made him famous throughout the world, including Russia, but the later Wells who was a campaigner for the idea of a world state in the 1920s and 1930s. In an often-cited letter to Kethevan Roberts of 18 May 1931, Huxley states that 'I am writing a novel about the future – on the horror of the Wellsian Utopia and a revolt against it' (Huxley [1946] 1979: 248). Similarly, it is in the writings of the later H. G. Wells that Orwell detects the machine worship of which he is so critical. He points out that 'in any book by anyone who feels at home in the machine-world – in any book by H. G. Wells, for instance – you will find passages of the same kind'. There the society of the future 'is envisaged as an ever more rapid march of mechanical progress', with 'machines to save work, machines to save thought, machines to save pain, hygiene, efficiency, organization, more hygiene, more efficiency, more organization, more machines–until finally you land up in the by now familiar Wellsian Utopia, aptly caricatured by Huxley in *Brave New World*' (Orwell [1937] 1971: 169).

This raises the question of Orwell's own attitude towards machinery and the idea of a fully automated machine society. Was he anti-machine and machinery? Orwell does occasionally suggest that he is. For example, in words that could have come from the writings of the young Marx on alienation, he says at one point that 'it is only in our own age, when mechanization has finally triumphed, that we can actually feel the tendency of the machine to make a fully human life impossible'. There is, he maintains, 'probably no one capable of thinking and feeling' who has not occasionally 'reflected that the machine is the enemy of life'. Orwell states that this feeling is usually 'instinctive rather than reasoned' (Orwell [1937] 1971: 167). He implies that his intention is to provide it with a rational foundation. In Orwell's own words, 'my job here is to supply the logical steps' in support of that conclusion which 'are usually left out' by those who rightly hold this view (Ibid.: 166).

Nevertheless, although he did not approve of machine worship, Orwell was not blind to the evident benefits to humanity that machinery or automation can bring about. He observes that 'everyone who is not a fool knows that it is nonsense to talk at this moment about scrapping the machine' (Orwell Ibid.: 165). He argues that it is necessary to be cautious about any 'anti-scientific bias', or a general 'hostility to science and machinery'. In particular we should, he argues. 'disregard the jealousy' of those, like Jonathan Swift, who hate science 'because science has stolen literature's thunder' (Ibid.: 166).

Orwell evidently thought that what is desirable is a position that lies somewhere between machine worship, on the one hand, and an attitude to outright hostility towards or rejection of machinery on the other. In other words, in his view, although there is definitely a place for machinery and indeed for industrial civilization in his understanding of what is a good life for human beings, nevertheless science and technology, economic progress and industrial development should be regarded as a means to an end. They are not and ought not to be regarded, as he thought they were in the Soviet Union, as ends in themselves. On this issue Orwell was in agreement with Aldous Huxley, who in the Foreword to the second edition of *Brave New World* (1946) maintains that in any revised vision of future society 'science and technology would be used as though' they 'had been made for man', not 'as though man were to be adapted and enslaved to them' (Huxley [1946] 1979: 9; Huxley [1959] 1983: 8–9).

A central feature of the fully automated machine society of the future that is identified by Orwell is technocracy. Orwell himself does not use that term. Rather, he tends to follow James Burnham, in his book *The Managerial Revolution*, by referring to the phenomenon of managerialism (Burnham [1942] 1944; Orwell [1947] 1968). The rulers of this future society, Burnham suggests, will be 'the people who effectively control the means of production', even if they do not strictly speaking own them. They will be members of a new ruling class comprising 'business executives, technicians, bureaucrats and soldiers', all of whom are 'lumped together by Burnham, under the name of "managers"'. Orwell notes that the technocratic society of the future that is organized in this way will not be 'in any accepted sense of the word, democratic'. For decision-making at all levels will be top-down and not bottom-up (Ibid.: 192). Burnham's thesis in *The Managerial Revolution* is evidently important for any understanding of Orwell's *Nineteen Eighty-Four*. Indeed, it lies at the heart of the views which are expressed in 'Goldstein's Testament' in that work.

A commitment to technocracy, or to what Orwell characterizes as managerialism, is a core feature of the thought of the later H. G. Wells. It is also one of the main targets of Zamyatin's critique of Wells' version of scientific utopianism in *We*. Both Wells and Zamyatin have in mind a latter-day form of Platonism, according to which in modern society the Guardian philosophers of Plato's *Republic* have been replaced by scientists, technicians and engineers. From the standpoint of enthusiasts for technocracy like H. G. Wells, it is not philosophy but rather science which will provide the solution to all of humanity's problems. The difference between Wells and Zamyatin is that, unlike Zamyatin, Wells was enthusiastic about this idea.

As Orwell freely acknowledged, his critique of the scientific utopianism of H. G. Wells owed a great deal to Zamyatin's *We*, as well as to Huxley's *Brave New World* (Orwell [1946] 1968; Orwell [1949] 1968). For example, like Zamyatin, Orwell suggests that in future society, whether capitalist or communist, 'everything that is now made of leather, wood, or stone' will 'be made of rubber, glass, or steel' (Orwell [1937] 1971: 166). Orwell regarded Zamyatin's *We* as both a commentary on and a critique of the Wellsian scientific utopia, with its notion of a technocratically managed machine society. In a review of Zamyatin's novel, written in 1946, Orwell argues that *We* 'is in effect a study of the Machine, the genie that man has thoughtlessly let out of its bottle and cannot put back again' (Orwell [1946] 1968: 99). He states that Zamyatin's novel, like that of Huxley. should be regarded as a negative reaction to the Wellsian idea of a 'rationalised, mechanised, painless world' (Ibid.: 96). It too 'debunks the super-rational, hedonistic type of Utopia' that we find in the writings of H.

G. Wells, something which, rightly or wrongly, both Zamyatin and Orwell associated with the vision of the machine society of the future which was embraced by the Russian Communist Party in the early 1920s (Orwell [1949] 1968: 546–7).

Orwell maintains that in *We* Zamyatin 'did not intend the Soviet regime', in particular, 'to be the special target of his satire'. After all, he observes, 'writing at about the time of Lenin's death, he (Zamyatin) cannot have had the Stalin dictatorship in mind'. Moreover, 'conditions in Russia in 1923 [*sic*] were not such that anyone would revolt against them on the ground that life was becoming too safe and comfortable'. In fact, 'what Zamyatin seems to be aiming at is not any particular country' but, rather, 'the implied aims of industrial civilisation in general' (Orwell [1946] 1968: 99). There is something to be said for this view. It remains the case, however, that, as we shall see in Part Two, at least some of developments which are the subjects of Zamyatin's critique in *We* existed in the Soviet Union as well as in the United States. It does not seem unreasonable to claim, therefore, that because Zamyatin did indeed intend to question the values of a fully automated machine society, and the alleged benefits of industrial civilization in general, it follows that he must also have intended to question the desirability of their introduction into the society of post-revolutionary Russia.

Part Two: Utopian Science Fiction: The Idea of a Fully Automated Machine Society in Marxism after Marx

I now turn to consider the views of Marxists in the Soviet Union at the beginning of the twentieth century regarding the idea of a fully automated machine society in the future. So far as this issue is concerned, Orwell's remarks about 'machine worship' in *The Road to Wigan Pier* are corroborated by Richard Stites in his influential work, *Revolutionary Dreams: Utopian Vision and Experimental Life in the Russian Revolution* (Stites 1989). In what follows I rely heavily at times on this work, although not uncritically. According to Stites, 'one of the most remarkable experiments to emerge from the Russian Revolution, fascinating in its vision and menacing in its ambition, was the cult of the machine'. In the 1920s 'the prophets of this cult' dreamed of 'remodelling human society along the lines of machine and workshop' (Stites 1989: 145).

Stites argues that the population of Russia at this time, especially its intelligentsia, 'glorified science and worshipped machines' (Stites 1989: 145). Like the scientist, and the technician, so too 'the engineer' was 'a hero of popular culture'. For the Russian reading public, 'science and technology provided a very compelling inspiration for speculative fiction'. Stites argues that the 'wedding of scientific and technological achievement to science fiction' was 'a natural one in this milieu'. The 'cult of the machine' and 'the image of an electrified nation' was prevalent in 'the arts' as well as in 'the political discourse of the age' (Ibid.: 169). Stites refers to the enthusiasm which the Bolsheviks in Russia had 'for technology, electricity, giant production units, machines, and the human machinery of a disciplined work force and an army' (Ibid.: 52).

Perhaps the clearest and best example of this cultural phenomenon is a two-volume work written by Alexander Bogdanov, one of Lenin's main Bolshevik opponents at the beginning of the twentieth century, namely *Red Star: A Utopia* (1908) and *Engineer Menni* (1913), both of which are works of utopian science fiction (Bogdanov [1908] 1984; Bogdanov [1913] 1984). As Stites has pointed out, Bogdanov's novels had a widespread appeal in Russia, both before and after the Revolution of 1917 (Stites 1984; Stites 1989: 32–3). Stites notes that

Bogdanov's *Red Star* 'was reprinted many times and enjoyed a huge circulation' after the Revolution of 1917 and that it 'served as the foundation stone for Soviet science fiction in the 1920s' (Stites 1989: 33). He also points out that Bogdanov lay at the heart of a 'Marxist counter-movement to Lenin's official Bolshevism in the years before World War I' (Ibid.: 33). Bogdanov is usually thought to be of interest because he was one of Lenin's targets for criticism in his *Materialism and Empiriocriticism: Critical Comments on a Reactionary Philosophy* (Lenin [1908] 2010). For present purposes, however, he is of interest for a different reason, namely his disagreement with Lenin over the issue of technocracy.

We saw earlier that George Orwell, following Yevgeny Zamyatin and Aldous Huxley, associated machine worship, and the vision of the society of the future as a fully automated society, with the writings of H. G. Wells. It is worth pointing out, therefore, that Wells and his ideas had a considerable influence on the Russian intelligentsia at the turn of the nineteenth and twentieth centuries. According to Stites, Wells 'enjoyed enormous popularity in Russia at the time' (Stites 1984: 4). It should also be noted that H. G. Wells twice visited Russia in his capacity as a journalist, writing up his experiences in a work entitled *Russia in the Shadows*, which he published in 1920. On his second visit Wells interviewed Lenin in Moscow (Wells 1920: 134–6; Stites 1989: 41–5). It was in that year that Lenin made his well-known remark that 'communism is Soviet power plus the electrification of the whole country' (Lenin [1920] 2012: 516). It was also in that year that Zamyatin wrote *We*.

Lenin's vision of the fully automated society of the future was similar to that of H. G. Wells in at least some respects. It was a vision of an advanced, industrial, urbanized society, a clean world of glass and chromium steel, powered by electricity, which would bring light as well as enlightenment to the Russian people. In that vision Russia is seen as entering the modern world. The model for this vision was arguably the United States, as epitomized by the architectural rational, scientific planning of the city of New York – the layout of its street system on the ground and of its skyscrapers, reaching to the heavens, or at least out to space. This was a Wellsian vision. It was also the vision of future society that was satirized by Zamyatin in *We*.

In *Russia in the Shadows* Wells refers to Lenin as 'the dreamer in the Kremlin' (Wells 1920: 123–44). He evidently considered Lenin to be a utopian thinker like himself. Despite Lenin's reputation as an orthodox Marxist, and ostensibly therefore a critic of all forms of utopianism, Wells observes that Lenin 'has succumbed at last to a Utopia, the Utopia of the electricians', which once it has come into being will bring with it 'a new and happier Communist' form of 'industrialism' (Wells 1920: 135). Wells maintains that Lenin had a 'vision of a world changed over and planned and built afresh' (Wells 1920: 138). In Lenin's dream of future society the 'decaying railways' system in Russia is 'replaced by a new electric transport'. Lenin 'sees new roadways spreading throughout the land' (Wells 1920: 135–6). Commenting on his interview with Lenin in 1920, Wells observes (with tongue in cheek) that 'while I talked to him he almost persuaded me to share his vision' (Ibid.: 136). This remark is not too surprising. For the vision of future society which Wells attributed to Lenin here was in fact his own.

Perhaps the best illustration of Lenin's vision of future society in Russia is provided by his remarks about electrification in his 'Report on the Work of the Council of People's Commissars', delivered on 22 December 1920. In his Report, Lenin asserts that it is necessary to adopt a 'broad economic plan' that is aimed at 'restoring our entire economy and raising it to the level of up-to-date technical development' within the world economy at that time, as exemplified by the capitalist societies of Europe and the United States. He argues that there is a need 'to place the economy of the country, including agriculture, on a new technical basis, that of modern large-scale production'. It is for this reason, he argues, that electrification is so important. For 'only electricity provides that basis' (Lenin [1920] 2012: 516).

A number of Russian Marxists writing at the beginning of the twentieth century, including both Lenin and Bogdanov, thought that the idea of a fully automated machine society, provided it is communist, could in principle be a good thing. However, they disagreed fundamentally with one another regarding the issue of how that society should be organized, at both the macro level of the state and the micro level of industrial relations within the Soviet economy. So far as the factory as a social institution is concerned, the question was, 'who ought to possess the authority to make decisions regarding the day-to-day organization of the production process there?' Should this be the workers themselves, either directly or through their elected representatives, as Alexandra Kollontai and the members of The Worker's Opposition movement argued at the time (Brinton 2004; Castoriadis 1993; Kollontai [1921] 1975), or should it be their unelected managers?' In short, the issue about which they disagreed was that of technocracy or managerialism versus industrial democracy.

Discussion of this issue in Russia at the beginning of the twentieth century was greatly influenced by the writings of Charles Winslow Taylor ([1911] 1998), whose *The Principles of Scientific Management* was published in the United States in 1911. Taylor was one of the main sources of theoretical inspiration for the Technocracy Movement and its scientific utopianism in America in the early twentieth century (Akin 1977; Bogulslaw 1965; Elsner jnr. 1967; Meier 1970; Segal 1985; Sibley 1971). His views regarding industrial relations had a considerable influence in both the United States and Europe (Drury 1915; Nelson 1980). However, what is more interesting for present purposes is that Taylor's notion of scientific management also had an impact on the intelligentsia in Russia.

Taylor's technocratic approach to industrial relations was the focus of a heated debate within the Bolshevik Party in the period after the Revolution of 1917 (Bailes 1977; Bailes 1978; Smith 1983; Sochor 1981). Richard Stites notes that although the 'labour movements' in Russia 'everywhere opposed Taylorism' because of what they regarded as its exploitative character, nevertheless 'it attracted a large segment of leftist intellectuals', especially those 'latter day St. Simonians who admired the organization, power, and discipline more than the socialism, equality, and justice of that tradition' (Stites 1989: 146). According to Stites, referring to the cult of machine worship in Russia in the 1920s, 'the prophets of this cult' were 'inspired by the industrial geniuses, Frederick Winslow Taylor and Henry Ford' in the United States and, like Taylor and Ford, dreamed of 'remodelling human society along the lines of machine and workshop' (Ibid.: 145).

Stites points out that, 'during the Revolution, numerous Bolsheviks were attracted by Taylorism's exaltation of efficiency and organization'. Lenin, in particular, 'was explicit about the need to adopt Taylor-like methods of labour organization, piece work, progressive wages, scientific management, and one-man control' over the production process (Ibid.: 147). On the issue of labour discipline, decision-making and authority within the factory, Stites claims that Lenin's views were 'unambiguous'. Despite his earlier reservations regarding Taylorism before the Russian Revolution (Lenin [1913] 1978; Lenin [1914] 2011), after it he became an ardent enthusiast for the idea of applying Taylor's ideas to the organization of labour in the factories of post-revolutionary Russia (Scoville 2001; Traub 1978). He believed that, at the micro level of the factory, 'the economy could not be maintained' by self-administering workers. Consequently, he resisted the idea of workers' control and 'promoted discipline, organization, the use of specialists, division of labour, and inequality in privilege'. Richard Stites points out that 'workers' control', 'anarchism', 'syndicalism' and democratic intraparty opposition were all 'repudiated by the Bolshevik leadership' at this time (Stites 1989: 44).

Although he did not use the term, Lenin defended the idea of technocratic decision-making by experts, that is to say, scientists, technicians and engineers. Lenin maintains in his Report that the present conjuncture in Russia 'marks the beginning of that very happy time' when politics 'will be discussed less often' and 'engineers and agronomists will do most of the talking' (Lenin [1920] 2012: 513–14). For it is from such technically mind people that 'we can really learn the business of economic development', the pursuit of which he insisted (implausibly) was a purely technical rather than a political issue (Ibid.: 514). Lenin states that the economic plan that he has in mind for the electrification of the country has been drawn up with the assistance of the technical expertise of the 'two hundred of our best scientific and technical men' who 'have worked on it' (Ibid.: 516). He states that 'our best men, our economic experts' have 'accomplished the task we set them of drawing up a plan for the electrification of Russia and the restoration of her economy' (Ibid.: 518).

Another enthusiast for technocracy and for Taylorism in Russia at this time was Aleksei Gastev (1882–1939). According to Stites, Gastev (writing in 1919) 'described a mechanized, standardized world, in a literal sense, with production ruled by self-regulating and self-correcting machines, joined throughout the world in a machine city – that is, a single unbroken mechanized civilization stretching around the globe' (Stites 1989: 152). Stites argues that Gastev's vision may be regarded as 'the ultimate version of the technocratic society' in Russia at the beginning of the twentieth century (Ibid.: 151). Central to this vision of a fully automated machine society was an emphasis on 'control, authority over the workers, discipline, labour draft, compulsion, rationing, piece rates – in short, the Taylor system' (Ibid.: 151). Although, in one sense of the term, Taylor's technocratic approach to decision-making might be said to be 'utopian' (Bogulslaw 1965; Segal 1985), nevertheless as an approach to labour relations it was inherently anti-democratic.

One reason for mentioning Gastev in this connexion is because his vision of the communist society of the future, as a fully automated machine society, together with his enthusiasm for Taylorism, was one of the main targets of criticism for Zamyatin in *We*. As Stites rightly observes, Zamyatin's novel 'presented a robust criticism of the idea of a machine society, as envisaged by Gastev and other Taylorists in Russia, including Lenin' (Stites 1989: 147; Bailes 1977; Beauchamp, 1983; Carden 1987; Rhodes 1976).

Zamyatin was not the only critic of technocratic scientific utopianism in Russia at this time. Of particular interest here is the contribution to the debate about the merits or otherwise of Taylorism which was made by Bogdanov in *Red Star* and *Engineer Menni*. Bogdanov is usually discussed in connection with his disagreement with Lenin about questions of metaphysics and the philosophy of science. From our point of view, however, he is of interest because of the account that he offers in his two novels of labour relations and decision-making within the factory in the communist society of the future. As Zenovia A. Sochor has argued, Bogdanov 'opposed Lenin on an array of questions, including Taylorism' (Sochor 1981: 248).

Bogdanov's ideas are quite close to those of George Orwell's Bolshevik machine worshippers on at least some issues. In *Red Star* he envisages the communist society of the future as being entirely mechanized and urbanized. In that society factories are 'operated by electric power and fully automated' (Stites 1989: 152; Stites 1984: 7). He also states that 'the soul of this formidable mechanism', in the fully automated factory of the future, will not be 'the crude force of fire and steam' but, rather, 'the fine yet even mightier power of electricity' (Bogdanov [1908] 1984: II, 2, 63). Moreover, in that society, economic production, at both the macro and the micro levels, will be organized in accordance with a 'plan' and, as such, will be 'calibrated by data-retrieval machinery and proto-computers' (Stites 1989: 33).

However, Bogdanov also introduces into his novel ideas that do not fit so readily with the technocratic vision of some of the other Bolsheviks, including Gastev and Lenin. As Stites notes, much like Zamyatin, Bogdanov regarded Gastev's Taylorist vision, in particular, to be 'inhuman' (Stites 1989: 152). According to Kendall Bailes, Gastev had maintained that in the communist society of the future 'the workers themselves would become increasingly mechanized and standardized, like cogs in a vast machine' (Bailes 1977: 378). Unlike Karl Marx, however, Gastev thought that this would be a good thing and not a bad one. In his opinion, it was not at all a nightmare scenario to be avoided but, rather, a positive societal ideal which ought to be pursued. Bailes notes that Bogdanov 'was repelled' by Gastev's 'attempt to reduce society to a vast machine and its members to unequal parts' (Ibid.: 379). Similarly, Richard Stites has noted that Bogdanov and other Bolshevik critics of Taylorism argued that this approach to industrial relations 'turned the worker into an ox or an automaton' (Stites 1989: 147).

Bogdanov objected strongly to Gastev's vision of 'an elite of engineers, standing above the proletariat and controlling it completely' (Bailes 1977: 380). In Bogdanov's more egalitarian and democratic vision of the communist society of the future, as envisaged in *Red Star* and *Engineer Menni*, 'rank and deference', that is to say social hierarchy within the factory, would 'not exist', nor would there be any 'coercive and authoritarian norms' (Stites 1989: 33). Richard Stites has noted that in a reply to Gastev, written in 1919, Bogdanov argued that in future society 'proletarian cooperation' and 'comradely recognition of competence' would 'replace authority and force in the workplace'. According to Bogdanov, within the factories of that future society 'leadership roles would be rotated according to the task and the talent' (Stites 1984: 8).

Stites maintains that in Bogdanov's vision of the future 'short workdays and the rotation of jobs' would 'reduce the menace of alienation and psychic enslavement to the machine' (Stites 1984: 7). Although Bogdanov certainly valued machines, nevertheless, like Marx, he 'feared and hated the system of capitalist production that made human beings appendages to machinery' (Ibid.: 7). Hence he was a staunch critic of the Taylor System, and of the Bolshevik followers of Taylor, especially Gastev, who was 'the greatest proponent of man-the-machine mentality' (Ibid.: 7). As the young Marx had envisaged in the 1840s, in his theory of alienation in the *Paris Manuscripts*, Bogdanov believed that in the communist society of the future machines could and would exist for the benefit of human beings, and not the other way around. This is a view which, as we saw earlier, can also be found in the writings of the authors of the great works of dystopian literature, including Aldous Huxley and George Orwell.

That Bogdanov was concerned about the issue of technocracy versus workplace democracy is clear from the fact that he introduced the debate surrounding it into his *Engineer Menni* (1913), which was a continuation of the ideas set out earlier in *Red Star*. The engineer Menni is portrayed by Bogdanov as a technocrat par excellence. As such, he is opposed on principle both to the excessive influence of independent trade unions and to the associated notion of workplace democracy. He is presented as someone who, like Lenin, thinks that decision-making should be placed in the hands of an intellectual elite of experts, that is to say scientists and engineers, who understand the science which ought to lie behind and inform them. Those who are not members of this intelligentsia are presented as being incapable of grasping the complexities of the science that is involved (Bogdanov [1913] 1984: II, 1, 186–7). In *Engineer Menni* it is Menni's son, Netti, who defends the idea of workplace democracy. In his opinion, democracy and technocracy are incompatible with one another, as also are socialism and technocracy. For socialism, properly understood, is inherently democratic (Bogdanov [1913] 1984: III, 1, 193–4).

Stites suggests that *Engineer Menni* is 'especially a novel about engineers' and 'technological heroes dominate this book'. The character Menni is an 'engineer of genius, master of planning and efficiency'. Moreover, his son Netti, like Bogdanov himself, 'devotes his later life to an encyclopedic study of work and an all embracing science of organization' (Stites 1984: 12). Stites suggests that the views of Menni and his son Netti, as presented in Bogdanov's novel, are essentially the same, that is to say, that their respective viewpoints are equally technocratic. This reading overlooks the disagreement that exists between the two characters regarding workplace democracy which Bogdanov took care to introduce into the text.

If Orthodox Marxists in Russia were critical of Bogdanov, one reason for this is that he had some sympathy for the criticisms of technocracy and of Taylorism which were being advanced by at least some Bolsheviks at this time. According to Kendal Bailes, Bogdanov 'accused' Gastev in particular 'of fostering a new elite of engineers' (Bailes 1977: 380). Zenovia A. Sochor has argued that Bogdanov's main criticism of Gastev was that his scheme 'lent itself to the rise of a new "social group" of educated engineers' who would be the key decision makers in industry. It is they who 'would perform creative, original functions' against a general 'background' of 'mass uniformity', and of passivity on the part of the majority of the workers, something to which Bogdanov was opposed (Sochor 1981: 259).

It is interesting to compare and contrast Bogdanov's *Red Star* with Zamyatin's *We*. The relationship between the two texts is a complex one. As Kathleen Lewis and Harry Weber have noted, there are some striking similarities between them (Lewis and Weber [1975] 2012: 188, 200). Given that Bogdanov was a member of the Bolshevik Party, it is possible that Zamyatin's *We* might be regarded as a satirical critique of Bogdanov's utopian vision of the communist society of the future in *Red Star*. Richard Stites has claimed that *We* was intended by its author to be 'an emphatic repudiation of Bogdanov's utopia – its technology and its rationalism, as well as its version of socialism' (Stites 1984: 14). This remark suggests that, in Stites's opinion, Zamyatin was critical of everything that Bogdanov stands for in his novel. After all, Bogdanov was closely associated with the idea of *Proletkult*, something to which Zamyatin was strongly opposed (Lewis and Weber [1975] 2012: 188). And yet things are not so simple as this. For that reading overlooks the existence of disagreements within Russian Marxism at the beginning of the twentieth century regarding the possible future direction of Russian society, especially the disagreement that existed between the views of Bogdanov and those of Lenin. Here I am not thinking about the philosophical disagreement that existed between these two thinkers. Rather, I have in mind their disagreement regarding the issue of technocracy and workplace democracy. Zamyatin would I think have approved of at least some of Bogdanov's ideas, especially his criticisms of Taylorism managerialism and technocracy.

When discussing these issues it is necessary to distinguish between the views of Marxists after Marx, especially in post-revolutionary Russia, and those of Marx himself. Richard Stites has argued that for Lenin 'the factory was the highest form of capitalist cooperation uniting and disciplining the proletariat'. Indeed, Lenin's enthusiasm for technology 'made him envision society' as a whole as just one 'vast office or factory'. According to Stites, Lenin had a technocratic vision which was 'rooted' in the writings of 'St. Simon and Marx' (Stites 1989: 44). In my view, however, it is questionable whether Stites's criticisms of Lenin do apply to Marx. As I have pointed out elsewhere (Burns 2024), there is evidence that Marx's views regarding the machine society of the future, for example in his 'Fragment on Machines' in the *Grundrisse* (1857–8), were indeed technocratic. However, there is also at least some evidence, especially in Marx's discussion of decision-making within the factory in *Capital*, volume 1 (1867), of a commitment on Marx's part to the idea that democracy or 'citizenship' in the workplace is one of the necessary preconditions overcoming alienation. If Marx is read in that way, then it might be argued that, so far as the Russian debate is concerned, it was Bogdanov and not Lenin who was closest to the more considered views about the significance of automation for labour relations within the factory that were held by Marx in *Capital*, volume 1.

Conclusion

The focus of this chapter has been on what has been said about the human consequences of automation or the introduction of new technology or machinery. A number of authors have suggested that this is alienating or dehumanizing. A fully automated machine society would be a completely alienated and dehumanized one. Some of those who have argued along these lines in the twentieth century were creative writers, specifically the authors of works of science fiction. However, such criticism has also been advanced by a number of theorists working within the Marxist tradition, including not least Marx himself. It is ironic, therefore, that the authors of the works of dystopian literature discussed in Part One of the chapter should have associated Marx and Marxism with technocratic utopianism. In so doing, they identified Marxism with Leninism and overlooked the existence of an alternative Marxist tradition, the members of which held views about the significance of automation which were in some respects very similar to their own. The issues addressed by these authors, Marxist and non-Marxist alike, retain their significance for us, in the world of AI and computing technology today.

References

Akin, W. E. (1977), *Technocracy and the American Dream: The Technocracy Movement: 1900–41*, Berkeley, CA: University of California Press.

Amis, K. ([1960] 2000), *New Maps of Hell: A Survey of Science Fiction*, North Stratford, NH: Ayer.

Armytage, W. H. G. (1968), *Yesterday's Tomorrows: An Historical Survey of Future Societies*, London: Routledge.

Bailes, K. E. (1977), 'Alexei Gastev and the Soviet Controversy over Taylorism', *Soviet Studies*, 29 (3): 373–94.

Bailes, K. E. (1978), *Technology and Society under Lenin and Stalin: Origins of the Soviet Technical Intelligentsia: 1917–1941*, Princeton NJ: Princeton University Press.

Beauchamp, G. (1983), 'Man as Robot: The Taylor System in Zamyatin's *We*', in Richard D. Erlich and Thomas P. Dunn (eds), *Clockwork Worlds: Mechanized Environments in SF*, 85–93, Westport, CT: Greenwood Press.

Benanav, A. (2020), *Automation and the Future of Work*, London: Verso.

Bogdanov, A. ([1908] 1984), 'Red Star: A Utopia', in A. Bogdanov (ed.), *Red Star: The First Bolshevik Utopia*, trans. Charles Rougle, ed. Loren R. Graham and Richard Stites, 17–140, Bloomington and Indianapolis: Indiana University Press.

Bogdanov, A. ([1913] 1984), 'Engineer Menni: A Novel of Fantasy', in A. Bogdanov (ed.), *Red Star: The First Bolshevik Utopia*, 141–234.

Bogulslaw, R. (1965), *The New Utopians*, Englewood Cliffs, NJ: Prentice Hall.

Brinton, M. (2004), *The Bolsheviks and Workers' Control*, in M. Brinton and D. Goodway (eds), *For Workers' Power: The Selected Writings of Maurice Brinton*, 293–378, Chico, CA: AK Press.

Burnham, J. ([1942] 1944), *The Managerial Revolution: Or, What is Happening in the World Now*, London: Putnam & Co.

Burns, T. (2023), 'Marx's *Capital* and the Concept of Super-Exploitation', *Capital & Class*, 48 (1): 1–21.

Burns, T. (2024), 'Marx, Automation and the Politics of Recognition within Social Institutions', *Critique: Journal of Socialist Theory*, 52 (2): 357–78.

Carden, P. (1987), 'Utopia and Anti-Utopia: Aleksei Gastev and Evgeny Zamyatin', *The Russian Review*, 46 (1): 1–18.

Castoriadis, C. (1993), 'The Role of Bolshevik Ideology in the Birth of the Bureaucracy', in C. Castoriadis (ed.), *Political and Social Writings*, vol. 3: *1961–1979: Recommencing the Revolution: From Socialism to the Autonomous Society*, 89–105, trans. D. A. Curtis, Minneapolis MN: University of Minnesota Press.

Danaher, J. (2019), *Automation and Utopia: Human Flourishing in a World without Work*, Cambridge MA: Harvard University Press.

Drury, H. B. (1915), *Scientific Management: History and Criticism*, New York: AMS Press.

Elsner jnr., H. (1967), *The Technocrats: Prophets of Automation*, Syracuse, NY: Syracuse University Press.

Frey, C. B. (2020), *The Technology Trap: Capital, Labour, and Power in the Age of Automation*, Princeton NJ: Princeton University Press.

Fuchs, C. and Mosco, V., eds (2015), *Marx in the Age of Digital Capitalism*, Leiden: Brill.

Fisher, E. and Fuchs, C., eds (2015), *Reconsidering Value and Labour in the Digital Age*, Basingstoke: Palgrave Macmillan.

Hillegas, M. R. (1967), *The Future as Nightmare: H. G. Wells and the Anti-Utopians*, New York: Oxford University Press.

Huxley, A. ([1931] 1938), 'The New Romanticism', in *Music at Night and Other Essays*, 211–20, Harmondsworth: Penguin Books.

Huxley, A. ([1946] 1979), *Brave New World,* London: Granada.

Huxley, A. ([1959] 1983), *Brave New World Revisited*, London: Panther Books.

Kassem, S. (2024), *Work and Alienation in the Platform Economy*, Bristol: Bristol University Press.

Kollontai, A. ([1921] 1975), *The Workers' Opposition in Russia*, London: Routledge.

Lenin, V. I. (1962–70), *Collected Works* in 50 vols, Moscow: Foreign Languages Publishing House.

Lenin, V. I. ([1908] 2010), *Materialism and Empiriocriticism: Critical Comments on a Reactionary Philosophy*, trans. Abraham Fineberg, ed. Clemens Dutt, in *Collected Works*, vol. 14: *1908*, Moscow: Progress Publishers.

Lenin, V. I. ([1913] 1978), 'A "Scientific" System of Sweating', *Collected Works*, vol. 18: *April 1912–March 1913*, 594–95.

Lenin, V. I. ([1914] 2011), 'The Taylor System: Man's Enslavement by the Machine', *Collected Works*, vol. 20: *December, 1913–August, 1914*, 152–54.

Lenin, V. I. ([1920] 2012), 'Report on the Work of the Council of People's Commissars (22 December, 1920)', *Collected Works*, vol. 31, *April–December 1920*, 487–518.
Lewis, K. and Weber, H. ([1975] 2012), 'Zamyatin's *We*: The Proletarian Poets and Bogdanov's *Red Star*', *Russian Literature Triquarterly*, 12: 253–78.
Marcuse, H. ([1977] 1978), *The Aesthetic Dimension: Towards a Critique of Marxist Aesthetics*, Boston, MA: Beacon Press.
Marx, K. ([1844] 1967), 'Estranged Labour', in *Economic and Philosophical Manuscripts of 1844*, 64–78, trans. Martin Milligan, London: Lawrence & Wishart.
Marx, K. ([1857–8] 1973), 'Fragment on Machines', *Grundrisse: Foundations of the Critique of Political Economy (Rough Draft)*, 692–714, trans. Martin Nicolaus, Harmondsworth: Penguin Books.
Marx, K. ([1867] 1974), 'Machinery and Modern Industry', *Capital: A Critical Analysis of Capitalist Production*, Part IV, chapter XV, 351–475, ed. Frederick Engels, trans. Samuel Moore and Edward Aveling, London: Lawrence & Wishart.
Meier, C. (1970), 'Between Taylorism and Technocracy: European Ideology and the Vision of Industrial Production in the 1920s', *Journal of Contemporary History*, 5 (2): 27–61.
Moylan, T. ([2000] 2018), *Scraps of the Untainted Sky: Science Fiction, Utopia, Dystopia*, London: Taylor & Francis.
Nelson, D. (1980), *Frederic W. Taylor and the Rise of Scientific Management*, Madison, WI: University of Wisconsin Press.
Orwell, G. (1968), *The Collected Essays, Journalism and Letters of George Orwell*, vol. 4, ed. S. Orwell and I. Angus, Harmondsworth: Penguin Books.
Orwell, G. ([1946] 1968), 'Review of *We* by E. I. Zamyatin', in *Collected Essays*, vol. 4, 95–9.
Orwell, G. ([1947] 1968), 'James Burnham and the Managerial Revolution', in *Collected Essays*, vol. 4, 192–215.
Orwell, G. ([1949] 1968), 'Letter to F. J. Warburg, 30th March, 1949', in *Collected Essays*, vol. 4, 546–7.
Orwell, G. ([1948] 1968), *Nineteen Eighty-Four*, Harmondsworth: Penguin.
Orwell, G. ([1937] 1971), *The Road to Wigan Pier*, Harmondsworth: Penguin.
Rhodes, C. H. (1976), 'Taylor's System of Scientific Management in Zamyatin's *We*', *Journal of General Education*, 28: 31–42.
Scoville, J. G. (2001), 'The Taylorization of Vladimir Illich Lenin', *Industrial Relations*, 40: 620–6.
Segal, J. P. (1985), *Technological Utopianism in American Culture*, Chicago, IL: University of Chicago Press.

Sibley, M. Q. (1971), *Technology and Utopian Thought*, Minneapolis, MN: Burgess Press.
Skidelsky, R. and Craig, N., eds (2020), *Work in the Future: The Automation Revolution*, New York: Palgrave Macmillan.
Smith, S. (1983), 'Taylorism Rules OK? Bolshevism, Taylorism and the Technical Intelligentsia in the Soviet Union 1917–41', *Radical Science Journal*, 13: 3–27.
Sochor, Z. A. (1981), 'Soviet Taylorism Revisited', *Soviet Studies*, 33 (2): 246–64.
Stites, R. (1984), 'Fantasy and Revolution: Alexander Bogdanov and the Origins of Bolshevik Science Fiction', in A. Bogdanov, *Red Star: The First Bolshevik Utopia*, trans. Charles Rougle, eds Loren R. Graham and Richard Stites, 1–16, Bloomington and Indianapolis: Indiana University Press.
Stites, R. (1989), *Revolutionary Dreams: Utopian Vision and Experimental Life in the Russian Revolution*, New York: New York University Press.
Susskind, D. (2021), *A World without Work: Technology, Automation and How We Should Respond*, London: Picador.
Taylor, F. W. ([1911] 1998), *The Principles of Scientific Management*, New York: Dover Books.
Traub, R. (1978), 'Lenin and Taylor: The Fate of "Scientific Management" in the (Early) Soviet Union', *Telos*, 37: 82–92.
Walsh, C. (1962), *From Utopia to Nightmare*, London: Bles.
Wells, H. G. (1920), 'The Dreamer in the Kremlin', in *Russia in the Shadows*, 123–44, London: Hodder & Stoughton.
Wendling, A. E. (2009), *Karl Marx on Technology and Alienation*, London: Palgrave Macmillan.
West, D. M. (2018), *The Future of Work: Robots, AI, and Automation*, Washington DC: Brookings Institution.
Zamyatin, Y. ([1920] 1972), *We*, trans. Bernard Guilbert Guerney, intro. Michael Glenny, Harmondsworth: Penguin Books.

8

Automation and the Good Life

Technological Enslavement, Technological Liberation or Technology Transformed?

Egidijus Mardosas

Introduction

Contemporary technological changes can leave one bewildered: what kind of life do they promise? Should we welcome or resist, for example, advances in Artificial Intelligence, virtual realities, robotics, gene therapies, artificially produced meat and other technologies? Many of us play with contemporary technologies such as Artificial Intelligence as if they were simply amusing tools, yet they have also become objects of intense speculation: while some propose that they will lead to an automated post-work utopia, others warn of their threats to humanity itself. The question of the nature of modern technologies and their impact on human well-being has become very sharp since the nineteenth century, with the advent of industrial capitalism and the rapid technological changes that followed. In this chapter, I discuss three theoretical positions with regard to the nature of technology: technology as an essentially neutral instrument that could be used to establish universal human flourishing; technology as an embodiment of an instrumentalist and reductionist relationship with the world that is destructive to human well-being; and a third position that can be called transformationalist, arguing that there is no technological essence as such and that technology can be many things.

I start by introducing the arguments of the optimists and the pessimists. A technological optimist would argue that contemporary technological developments prepare the ground for a much better society in which most of the grudging work will be eliminated and people will enjoy free, equal and leisurely lives. A pessimist sees in technology a dark force that enslaves humanity to the machine, transforms human relations under primitive utilitarian lines and destroys all that is meaningful in human lives. If an optimist sees in technology a promise of the truly good life, a pessimist observes a threat to the good life. I will argue that both positions remain too one-sided, and that we therefore need a third position: one that does not reject technology as a basis for the good life, but that refuses to take technology as it has developed under capitalist historical conditions as the only horizon. A transformationalist argues that technology itself can be transformed to express different sets of values. From such a position, the question of the relationship between technology and the good life can be posed anew.

The Technological Utopia

The most optimistic arguments about the liberatory potential of contemporary technologies can be found in the recent accelerationist arguments concerning a fully automated technological utopia. In this view, technological developments must be pushed forward as fast as possible so that everyone can live a life of leisure and freedom.

Nick Srnicek and Alex Williams, in their #Accelerate manifesto (2013), argue that contemporary progressive political forces must propose their own grand and brave imaginary of the good life, instead of simply opposing neoliberal capitalism. The vision of the good life that the authors propose is based on the technological achievements of capitalism, which, if taken over and put under collective control, could deliver universal prosperity. While they acknowledge the many problems, including the climate collapse, that contemporary societies are facing, they contend that these problems are not caused by technology itself, but by capitalism. To save ourselves from this predicament and deliver a future of universal human flourishing, we must push forward the development of technology. At the centre of this reasoning is the assumption that technological potentialities remain unrealized because of capitalist social relations. Getting rid of capitalist social relations will allow their technological basis to be used to deliver universal flourishing:

> Accelerationists want to unleash latent productive forces. In this project, the material platform of neoliberalism does not need to be destroyed. It needs to be repurposed towards common ends. The existing infrastructure is not a capitalist stage to be smashed, but a springboard to launch towards post-capitalism.
> (Srnicek and Williams 2013)

In their follow-up book, *Inventing the Future* (2016), Srnicek and Williams argue that progressive politics should be built around a post-work imaginary – that is, a vision of society where work is finally eliminated. For this, automation is central. Therefore, the authors encourage progressive political forces to embrace full automation as their central political demand. Full automation, together with universal basic income, should be employed to drastically shorten the working week and to liberate people to engage in other, more meaningful activities. An accompanying cultural shift is also necessary: the work ethic to which we have all become accustomed through centuries of capitalism should be rejected, and people should rebuild their lives around fulfilling forms of leisure and non-work instead of being controlled by the imperative of production.

Paul Mason, in his *PostCapitalism* (2015), contributes to these debates with the argument that the development of technologies, of which the most important are the information technologies, has already created a networked society full of sharing and cooperation which is destroying the foundations of capitalism. The technological achievements of capitalist societies are themselves pushing forward towards a post-capitalist society. Mason argues that contemporary technologies reduce the reproduction costs of various economic goods to near zero, thus destroying the price mechanisms of a capitalist economy. Capital becomes more and more parasitic, imposing artificial price controls and appropriating what is often produced by the cooperation of networked individuals. Thus, if we could only get rid of capital, which is increasingly becoming socially parasitic, we could finally unleash these technological forces of cooperation and have a truly post-capitalist society. This would create a post-scarcity society with a much shorter working day, where cooperation and sharing are encouraged and much more time is secured for individual development due to universal basic income, universal basic services and other schemes of redistribution.

Aaron Bastani takes over Mason's main argument that contemporary technologies are already destroying capitalist structures and that they promise 'a society in which work is eliminated, scarcity replaced by abundance and where labour and leisure blend into one another' (Bastani 2019: 50). Bastani argues for fully automated luxury communism for everyone. Such a society is made possible by technologies that automate human work, deliver cheap and clean energy, ensure human health and longevity and are, furthermore, environmentally sustainable. Most of the technologies that promise a luxurious post-work utopia are in their early stages already, all we need to do is to push their development and make them universally accessible – a question of politics, not of technology. Thus, Bastani, like Srnicek, Williams and Mason before him, calls for global democratic and anti-capitalist politics that would release these technological potentialities from capitalist constraints.

Technological optimists do not lack critical awareness of all the ways in which contemporary technologies are used to spy, control and oppress people or cause environmental destruction. Mason, for example, in his later book (Mason 2019) discusses various dangers of contemporary technologies. Yet even being critical of the various forms of oppression made possible by some contemporary technologies, the imagined future utopia is still based on largely the same technologies that are being developed now. The question is not technology itself, but to what ends it is used: contemporary information technologies can become tools of surveillance and oppression, or they can be used democratically for the collective coordination of production and distribution.

More examples can be given of the reasoning that the achievement of utopia ultimately rests on the technologies that might now be used for purposes that are not very benign. John Danaher (2019) argues that a world of full automation should be a virtual utopia, in which we would live mostly in virtual realities. For Danaher, this is a good thing: a virtual utopia could be a truly liberated world, where we could leave all practical concerns aside and immerse ourselves in virtual experiments that express our creative powers and desires. Another example can be found in Phil Jones's (2021) critique of contemporary forms of micro-work and platform work. Jones extrapolates the possibility of a utopia from the same forms of work that contemporary capitalism advocates, and his utopia is that of very little work which is distributed among society as micro-work. The technologies underlying such forms of work also survive in Jones's utopia. If, for example, algorithms are used to increase the speed of work and oppress the worker even more in capitalist societies, work in the post-work utopia is distributed using the same algorithms: 'Much as on micro-work sites, machine learning algorithms could be used to calculate and distribute available work, but in ways that privilege free time and autonomy' (Ibid.: 111). The gamification of work also persists: 'Review and score systems might, to some degree, succeed the wage as a means to motivate due effort. Instead of deciding who gets paid and who gets to survive, score systems might act as soft forms of encouragement, playful forms of competition, acting to gamify otherwise gloomy toil' (Ibid.: 112). Even in the future utopia work would remain surveyed and ranked, this time with the promise that such techniques might deliver more freedom and encourage mild and beneficial forms of competition.

The Technological Nightmare

A very different line of argument is also prominent in debates on the nature of technology: technology itself is perceived as a threat to human well-being. Such critiques highlight that technologies deliver a false promise of security, control and predictability, instead engendering oppression and destroying all that is meaningful and fulfilling in human existence. Therefore, we should not seek to accelerate technological development, but to resist it, and to defend human interactions and practices that constitute good and flourishing lives against the encroachment of modern technologies.

Early versions of this argument, proposed by Martin Heidegger in Germany and Jacques Ellul in France, rested on a highly charged metaphysical understanding of the nature of technology. For Heidegger (1977), technology is not neutral; it cannot be understood as a mere means but must be grasped in its essence. There is a fundamental break between the premodern technologies and the modern ones, according to Heidegger. The essence of modern technology lies in the way it reveals nature as a standing reserve, a resource for exploitation. Nature becomes only a storehouse of energy to be subjugated to human demands. This mode of revealing poses an 'unreasonable demand', forcing nature into an alien form instead of revealing its truth, its real essence (Ibid.: 14). Heidegger sees this mode of revealing nature spreading to human relations as well – for example, in the form of a 'human resources' approach. For Heidegger, the technical mode of revealing poses a danger to humanity, as the more it spreads, the more it blocks the way of revealing that does justice to the nature of things, which Heidegger calls poietic revealing.

Jacques Ellul (1964) based his critique on the concept of technique. Technique is not technology or machines, but a certain instrumentalist relationship marked by efficiency and rationalization. Technique prepares various activities for their mechanization: technique must first re-arrange them according to its principles, and then various tasks can be taken over by machines; thus, 'technique integrates machine into society' (Ibid.: 5). Ellul discusses how technique, as the rationalizing instrumentalist approach, spreads through society, subjecting different spheres of modern life under its sway: 'it ranges from the act of shaving to the act of organizing the landing in Normandy, or to cremating thousands of deportees' (Ibid.: 21). In the economy, technique produces capitalism, the enslavement of workers and the overall transformation of the human into *homo economicus*. Spreading to the state, technique creates propaganda machines and totalitarian forms of control; technique subjugates leisure time through mass media and creates consumerist societies, and so on – the overall effect being that humans behave more and more like cogs in a machine. Individual differences disappear together with individual autonomy and freedom, while those in power receive new tools to deliver unseen forms of destruction. At the very opening of his study, Ellul warns of the gravity of the danger of this phenomenon: 'At stake is our very life, and we shall need all the energy, inventiveness, imagination, goodness, and the strength we can muster to triumph in our predicament' (Ibid.: xxxii). While Ellul does not propose a solution to the problem of technology, he seeks to spread awareness of the danger. With this new awareness we can begin to look for solutions.

This train of thought, originally developed after the Second World War, is alive in more contemporary critiques, though in a less radical vein. In the 1980s it was reintroduced by Albert Borgmann (1984) with his distinction between a thing and a device. A thing is always situated and contextualized; approached with certain practices, it gathers people around itself, it has a world. A device, on the contrary, is much more abstract; it only provides a certain basic function to everyone (a commodity, in the terminology of Borgmann). He exemplifies this with the difference between a stove (a focal thing) and a central heating plant (a device):

> Thus a stove used to furnish more than mere warmth. It was a *focus*, a hearth, a place that gathered the work and leisure of a

family and gave the house a center [...] A device such as a central heating plant procures mere warmth and disburdens us of all other elements.

(Ibid.: 41–2, emphasis in the original)

Focal things and practices are therefore part of rich and meaningful interaction with the world, while technological devices are not. The more our lives become technologically mediated, the more we lose our focal practices and the more our lives become abstract, dull, lonely and meaningless. 'Technology ceaselessly transforms the world along abstract and artificial lines' (Ibid.: 29). Like for Heidegger before him, for Borgmann the spheres of meaning and technology are radically different.

The position from which Borgmann writes is highly conservative: a technological world has lost its true traditional values and delves into meaningless consumerism and permissiveness. Borgman is not advocating for a return to a pre-technological world, however. Instead, he thinks that the alienation and meaninglessness that we will supposedly experience will lead us to ask what constitutes good life and to acknowledge the importance of focal practices: 'if we recognize the central vacuity of advanced technology, that emptiness can become an opening for focal things' (Ibid.: 199). By becoming aware of the destructive nature of technological devices we can approach them consciously and carefully, finding them a proper place in our lives without confusing technology with those things and practices that are truly meaningful.

A much more recent variant of the pessimist argument can be found in James Bridle's *New Dark Age* (2018). As the title suggests, Bridle thinks that technological developments are leading us towards dark times. All our contemporary technologies, according to Bridle, are based on the principle of computation: on the assumption that various tasks can be approached as mathematical problems, divided into measurable elements and codified, and that their best solutions can be computed accordingly. This is the belief that more data and more computational power will make our interactions more transparent and more efficient, will reduce complexity and will expand our agency. All of this, according to Bridle, is an illusion. Our pursuit of technological mastery of the world leads to growing obscurity, confusion and loss of control: 'the more obsessively we attempt to compute the world, the more unknowably complex it appears' (Bridle 2018: 46). More and more data, faster and faster machines lead to a situation in which we lose our human abilities to make judgements and instead trust the machines to make decisions for us. To make matters worse, we also do not understand how the machines work. Here Bridle focuses on Artificial Intelligence and contemporary forms of automation to make his point: most of us have no idea how algorithms make decisions, we simply trust them. A much-loved example for Bridle is the Global Positioning System (GPS): by trusting the system, we lose our ability to orient in the world without it. The world becomes more obscure, while we become enslaved by machines: 'Arranging the world from the perspective of the machine renders it computationally efficient, but makes it completely incomprehensible to humans. And moreover, it accelerates their oppression' (Ibid.: 103).

From the position of the pessimist, the problem with technologies lies not in the ends for which they are used, but in the nature of technology itself, its underlying computational structure. Our actions in the world are simply far too complicated to be turned into mathematical problems with clearly defined variables and one optimal solution. Trusting that machines operate with such clearly defined variables and make neutral decisions, we lose sight of the fact that machines are biased: the world is forced into a yes/no paradigm, which reduces its essential complexity and leads to decisions that cannot but be biased. Therefore, our problems are not caused by, say, capitalist motives in technological rollout, but by technological expansion as such, although Bridle acknowledges that technological development is driven by 'military, government, and corporate interests' (Ibid.: 211). What is the solution to this conundrum? Like Borgmann, Bridle does not ask us to reject technology, but argues for 'a more thoughtful engagement with technology' (Ibid.: 17). We should treat technologies as often useful tools yet be aware of their limitations and ensure that we do not allow them to encroach on our agency too much. We should embrace the complexity and fragility of our agency. Instead of trusting machines, we must learn to trust our capacities, as imperfect as they are, to navigate the world. With this new awareness, new cooperation between humanity and machines will be possible, suggests Bridle.

The Primacy of the Forces of Production

Which perspective is more convincing? Are we being liberated or enslaved by contemporary technologies? I will address the optimist arguments first. As already observed, the central idea of the accelerationist optimist is that our technologies, as they have developed under capitalism, form the foundation for a better society. This argument has its clear origins: Karl Marx's *Preface to A Contribution to the Critique of Political Economy* (1859), where Marx introduced his base and superstructure model of social change. Like contemporary accelerationists, Marx encouraged the working classes not to struggle against the machines, but to take over their control to build a better society. The crux of Marx's argument in the

Preface is that the development of the forces of production reaches a point at which they come into conflict with the existing relations of production and cause social revolution, after which new relations of production are established that are more appropriate to the state of technological development. In Marx's own words:

> At a certain stage of development, the material productive forces of society come in conflict with the existing relations of production or – this merely expresses the same thing in legal terms – with the property relations within the framework of which they have operated hitherto. From forms of development of the productive forces these relations turn into their fetters. Then begins an era of social revolution.
>
> (Marx 1859)

Under this view, capitalism emerged because the development of the forces of production could no longer be contained within the feudal relations of production; capitalist relations of production have allowed rapid technological advance, yet this technological base can no longer be contained within capitalist relations. Instead, it starts to conflict with them and pushes us towards socialist relations of production that will be more appropriate for realizing the potentialities contained in the forces of production.

Marx's preface contains many strong claims about the development of human history: that the forces of production define what kind of social relations exists in human society, that human development is primarily driven by this technological basis and that social transitions happen only when the forces of production have reached their maximum possible development under given relations of production. This text remains highly controversial, even among Marxists, for its supposedly simplistic and deterministic explanation. While many

Marxists have attempted to offer more nuanced interpretations, the *Preface* has found its defenders, like G. A. Cohen, who offered the thesis that 'the development of the productive forces proceeds systematically, and production relations conform to that development' (Cohen 1978: 142), against more nuanced and multidirectional interpretations ('that zig-zag "dialectic"', in Cohen's words). Of course, Cohen allows some room for the relations to influence the forces, or for the systematic development of the forces to regress and stagnate temporarily, but he emphatically stresses that the overall direction is that of progress. Human history is the history of the progressive growth of our productive powers, which is the independent variable to explain the changes in social structures.

There is much in this reasoning to unpack, as it attempts to put all human history under one universal scheme of development. I am not suggesting that technological optimists subscribe to this scheme *in toto*, but we can see how one essential part of this structure underlies their reasoning: capitalist society has pushed technological development towards a point where a new kind of society can be established on this technological basis. Capitalism now only fetters the further realization of the utopian potential contained in the forces of production, and we need only change the social relations to realize this potentiality. The primacy of technology thesis suggests that the level of technological development defines the nature of utopia. For the pessimist, the same story is inverted: the history of technological development is the history of human degeneration, not of progress. What is needed is not to unleash technological potential further, but to contain it. For both optimists and pessimists, technology determines the nature of society: for the optimist, it points towards post-work utopia; for the pessimist, to human degeneration and enslavement under the machine.

Real Subsumption by Capital

To offer a comprehensive critique of the base and superstructure model falls outside the scope of this essay. It has been questioned, reinterpreted or discarded many times, yet an important impetus to question it again comes from contemporary eco-Marxist scholars, who also provide an alternative interpretation of the interaction between the forces and relations of production. Their interpretation checks the optimism of the accelerationist position. Given how the development of the productive forces under capitalism leads to the destruction of the natural environment to such an extent that it threatens to destroy human life as such, it becomes doubtful that this same development could create the technological basis for a better kind of society. Environmental destruction is not simply an issue of fossil fuels – as if all we need do is transition from fossil fuels to renewable energy and the destruction of ecosystems will disappear. Instead, repairing the relationship between humanity and other forms of life on earth requires fundamentally restructuring not only our technological basis but also our social relations and lifestyles. The whole idea of full automation then becomes problematic, as it rests on the assumption that the technologically intense lifestyle that has developed at the centres of capitalist production can be universalized. The environmental costs, even without fossil fuels, of universalizing such a form of life for 8 billion people will be enormous: more automation means more energy use, more machines means more rare earth minerals, thus more excavation, and so on. The challenges we are facing will not be solved with more (albeit 'greener') technologies, allowing us to keep our technologically intensive lifestyles, but with a dramatic rearrangement of the relationships between humanity and nature.

Marx has often been criticized from the ecological perspective for his productivist bias. However, ecological Marxism proposes a different reading of Marx, one that allows for a more complicated relationship between the technological base and the good life. Marx's distinction between the formal and the real subsumption of labour processes by capital, introduced in the *Economic Manuscripts of 1861–1863*, provides one source from which to reconceptualize the relationships between technology and social structures. When capital first appears historically, argues Marx, it has to contend with the process of labour (technologies, forms of labour and skills) as it exists, only taking control over it. Capital controls the process of production only formally, 'without making any changes in its specific technological character' (Marx 1988: 92). Eventually, capital reorganizes production according to its own needs: it destroys old structures of labour and changes the forces of production, introducing new technologies, new forms of labour, new power relations in the process of production, and so on. In the process, the forces of production become thoroughly transformed. Now, capital has truly subsumed the process of labour according to its needs.

In *Capital*, Marx also analysed how various technological inventions result from social struggles: on the one hand, due to demands to secure better working conditions for workers, for example, a safer technology is developed. On the other hand, Marx also shows how various technological developments were introduced in order to extract more labour from workers and to ensure better control of the labour process: 'It would be possible to write a whole history of the inventions, made since 1830, for the sole purpose of providing capital with weapons against working class revolt' (Marx 1990: 563). What this model points to is something very different from the previous model: it is the relations of production that transform the means of production. The more capitalism advances, the more it reorganizes society according to its own need for capital accumulation.

Focusing on Marx's discussion on real subsumption by capital, eco-Marxist thinker Kohei Saito challenges the productivist assumptions of the accelerationists. For Saito, Marx in his later life experienced a shift in his thinking. Once he understood the implications of his theory of real subsumption, he came to question his previous assumptions about the progressive development of technologies: 'Marx came to realize that the capitalist development of technologies does *not* necessarily prepare a material foundation for post-capitalism' (Saito 2023: 8). Capitalism encourages technological developments only with the interests of expanding the accumulation of capital and the continuation of capitalist relations of production. From the perspective of real subsumption, argues Saito further, the forces of production and the relations of production cannot easily be separated, as it becomes obvious that the forces of production are infused with a certain relationship. For example, large-scale production technologies require certain structures of command and control, machines are such that they destroy workers' skills and autonomy, and so on. The technological basis of capitalism is too strongly imbued with capitalist forms of labour process to be a basis for an alternative society. Technologies that destroy humans' skill, initiative and environment cannot be simply taken over for collective use as a basis for a better society (Ibid.: 158). This means that post-capitalist society will face the challenge of fundamentally reforming its technological basis according to its own set of values.

An Example: The Transition from Water to Coal

The process of real subsumption by capital is illustrated by Andreas Malm's study *Fossil Capital* (2016). Focusing on the early decades of the nineteenth century that marked the shift from water power to coal and the steam engine, Malm argues that this shift cannot be explained by some kind of technological rationality, as if the transition occurred because steam was simply more efficient and cheaper. He shows that the power capacity of waterwheels was no less than that of the steam engines of the time. There was also an abundance of high-quality locations for watermills that remained unused, and some impressive technological innovations were developed that significantly increased the capabilities of waterwheels. Furthermore, even the industrialists themselves understood the steam engine to be a very expensive investment that only brought problems (the cost and storage of coal, the cost of repairing the engine, etc.). Many industrialists were even outspoken critics of the steam engine, yet within a few short decades watermills disappeared and coal and steam became the norm. Malm's argument is that this can only be explained by class conflict: that the capitalists shifted to steam and coal during a very intense period of class struggle with a view to crushing the power of organized workers and imposing better control of production. With coal and steam, the production process was finally fully subsumed by capital: factories could now be built where people already were (instead of relying on pre-existing geographical conditions), the machines turned on and switched off at the whim of the capitalist and all fluctuations of production coming from the natural fluctuations of water power were eliminated with a fuel that could be transported and used in the quantities needed. Malm's argument shatters any simplistic base and superstructure model according to which technology is an independent variable and the development of productive forces causes the change in the superstructure. Here, it was the superstructural processes that influenced the course of technological development.

An important aspect of Malm's argument is that water power required at least some kind of cooperation between different enterprises and communities sharing the same water source. Water is not an individual source of power: factories need it, peasants need it, towns need it, and a fair sharing scheme must be implemented. Therefore, water was much less suited to individual competition among enterprises than coal, the supply and use of which can be fully controlled individually. On top of that, the industrial economy, argues Malm, was fully capable of further developments with water power. Some impressive new inventions made it possible to drastically increase the power of waterwheels and to even out the natural fluctuations of the water supply. The water-based economy was very far from reaching its technological limits of expansion. Of course, it could hardly keep up with the capabilities of fossil fuels in the longer run, but that is an argument from the future; at the time, a water power-based industrial economy was a real possibility. Thus, the choice between water and coal was also a choice between two types of industrial society: a cooperative one, where enterprises need to adjust their production with the broader needs of community; and an individualistic one based on the free competition of private capital.

Technology Transformed: Marcuse and Feenberg

This new perspective encourages scepticism regarding the arguments that contemporary technologies, as they have developed under capitalist historical conditions, could form the basis of an alternative society. Does this mean that the pessimists win the argument? Not necessarily, if we can make a better case for the possibility of alternative technology.

In his *Essay on Liberation* (1969), Herbert Marcuse proposed that science and technology, liberated from capitalist constraints and the instrumentalist outlook of the domination of nature, can be repurposed and reinvented in such a way that the contradiction between nature and technology, production and art, disappears. Instead of being a force of domination over nature, the technology of liberated society would be guided by the aesthetic concerns of free humanity. Such alternative technology would liberate nature and encourage its flourishing, and would also liberate human nature and allow the flourishing of human creative, aesthetic, moral, psychological, rational and other powers: 'The liberated consciousness would promote the development of a science and technology free to discover and realize the possibilities of things and men in the protection and gratification of life, playing with the potentialities of form and matter for the attainment of this goal' (Marcuse 1969: 24). Marcuse stressed that the difference between technique and art would disappear, and liberated humanity would be guided by aesthetic concerns, celebrating life as such.

Jürgen Habermas, however, was sceptical of such an idea of alternative technology that overcomes the division between technique and art. He argued that technology as such embodies a certain instrumentalist rationality. Technology can only be used for different purposes, yet in itself it always remains technology as we know it. For Habermas, technology is of course shaped by capitalist interests, yet at its deeper level it is still marked by an objectifying and controlling relationship with nature, irrespective of the purposes for which it is used. Technology, for Habermas, is 'a "project" of human species *as a whole*', which denies the possibility of radically alternative technology even in a radically alternative society (Habermas 1970: 87, emphasis in the original).

Andrew Feenberg, in his turn, was not fully convinced by Habermas's position. Critical of Marcuse's vision of harmony between nature and technology, he aims to defend an idea of alternative technology as encompassing different social values, challenging Habermas's approach (Feenberg 1996). At the centre of Feenberg's theory is the idea of two levels of rationalization that are embodied in technological devices. At the most basic level is technological rationality *à la* Habermas, which allows us to distinguish technological and non-technological actions. However, each device is shaped by a second level of rationalization that includes various social concerns and values. The first level does not define concrete technologies because this underlying technological rationality is always mediated by the second level. As a result, what we perceive as the essence of technology 'can only be the sum of all the major determinations it exhibits in its various stages of development' (Ibid.: 66). For Feenberg, the history of technological innovation is marked by various social struggles: capitalist interests have a dominating position, yet resistances have always been there, as well as various user experiments and innovations that ignore capitalist imperatives. Understood in this way, numerous possibilities for what technologies could be emerge.

Not only can technologies be used for different purposes, therefore, but an alternative set of values can be embedded in these devices, producing technologies that are effectively different from what we now understand to be the essence of technology. 'The design of technology is thus an ontological decision fraught with political consequences' (Feenberg 2002: 3). For Feenberg, it is essential that the users of technology influence the development of concrete devices. He calls for 'democratic transformations from below' (Ibid.: 17) that would incorporate interests and values that now remain supressed under the capitalist conditions of technological development. These values would be embedded in the technological devices themselves, thus sustaining different social relationships than exist under capitalism. The result would be no less than 'a general overhaul of technology' (Ibid.: 185). Technology could be redesigned to encourage a more sustainable relationship with nature, as well as supporting the development of human creative powers and capabilities. As such, deskilling, control and natural destruction are not necessarily guaranteed outcomes of technology: 'technology does not pose an insuperable obstacle to the pursuit of "humanistic" values' (Ibid.: 143).

The Aristotelian Principle

If the theory of real subsumption by capital allows the position of the techno-optimist to be questioned, then the possibility of alternative technology also allows the pessimistic position to be broken from. When we accept that technological devices can embody and sustain different values and different social relations, then the sharp division between the sphere of meaning and the sphere of technology, between a device and a focal thing, also becomes blurred. We are no longer faced with the prospect of only limiting technological intrusion into normatively governed areas of human life, but can also transform technologies to reflect and aid the realization of those values and ends that we find most important for the good life. The next question thus becomes: What kind of normative perspective should guide our attempts to transform technology? Feenberg introduced the idea of democratizing the process of technological innovation. Here I would propose that this can be supplemented with 'the Aristotelian principle', introduced to the philosophy of technology by Borgmann (who takes it from John Rawls).

As already mentioned, Borgmann was writing from a highly conservative position – for him, the horrors of a technological society included not only meaningless and exploitative forms of work and endless consumerism but also abortion, homosexuality, pornography and even liberal democracy itself. However, the idea of the Aristotelian principle should not be conflated with Borgmann's social views. For Borgmann, this principle means that the best life is a life of activity in which various human powers and capacities are exercised. The Aristotelian principle thus states that the good life does not consist simply of the satisfaction of immediate material needs, which can easily be achieved by technological advancement, but is primarily a matter of the quality and complexity of life.

The Aristotelian principle, as Borgmann discusses it, also includes the principle of complexity: 'The more complex the faculties to whose cultivation we are devoted, the more excellent our life' (Borgmann 1984: 211). While Borgmann criticizes the principles of liberalism, he recognizes that the Aristotelian principle also incorporates diversity: 'The good life, then, is one of engagement, and engagement is variously realized by various people' (Ibid.: 214). The unity of the principle of complexity with the principle of diversity is important to stress, as it differs from Aristotle's own thinking. Aristotle defended a hierarchy of human activities in which the life of reason is the best, while the life of manual work is the worst. The Aristotelian principle, as a normative principle guiding technological transformation, should include a much more diversified conception of the good life, in which various powers and capacities are actualized – not only reason but also various aesthetic, moral and creative capacities, with the good life consisting of engaging in a variety of activities that express these powers. This means that the good life can take many forms, there being no correct way of arranging various powers and capabilities.

Another important qualification of the Aristotelian principle concerns the relationships between work and human flourishing. Aristotle introduced a sharp distinction between the good life and the life of work, arguing that only those who do not need to work can lead flourishing lives. Aristotle used this argument to defend class oppression and to exclude working people from the best polis. Yet Aristotle's argument can also be used to argue that the realization of the good life requires that all people be liberated from unpleasant, tedious, debilitating forms of work. Therefore, the Aristotelian principle would welcome various technological developments that eliminate tedious and unpleasant work. On the other hand, forms of work that bring satisfaction, offer meaning and express various human powers do not contradict the Aristotelian principle as defined above. Therefore, from the perspective of the Aristotelian principle, the choice is not just between work and leisure but also between alienating and non-alienating forms of work.

Coda: An Epoch of Rest

At the end of the nineteenth century, two visions of a future liberated society confronted each other in the form of utopian novels written by two prominent writers and activists of the time. Edward Bellamy's *Looking Backward: 2000 – 1887* (1888) told the story of a future egalitarian society based on the technological achievements of capitalism. In this story, capitalism has concentrated the means of production and in this way has prepared the technological ground for a collectivist post-work society. These enormous productive capabilities are now used for providing all people with the necessities of life through a centrally planned production and distribution system. What little has remained of the necessary work is organized through work armies in which all participate equally. This is a well-organized, centralized, egalitarian, technological post-work society. Curiously, the transition happens without grand revolutionary struggles because eventually everyone, even the capitalists, realizes that the enormous, concentrated means of production have grown out of the capitalist constraints and are better used collectively. Here, with the already very familiar argument, technology, as it has developed under capitalism, has prepared the ground for a post-capitalist society.

For William Morris, a libertarian socialist, this was a totalitarian nightmare – a society run like a factory. Bellamy envisioned only a 'half-change', wrote Morris (2004: 354) in his review, and took an advanced capitalist city as an image of universal utopia, failing to acknowledge that you cannot have a better society without fundamentally restructuring its means of production. He immediately responded with his own utopia in *News from Nowhere or An Epoch of Rest* in 1889 (Morris 2004). If, for Bellamy, a good society is achieved by a reformist transition from capitalism to post-capitalism and built on capitalist technological grounds, for Morris it is realized through a long and arduous struggle against capital. In the end, people are victorious and reconstruct social relations on different principles. This is the time of rest, as the title indicates: people shake off the productivist culture of capitalism and focus on building meaningful lives. The grand industrial machine is disbanded, and overcrowded urban areas abandoned for a more decentralized lifestyle. People cultivate lifestyles based on freedom, equality and solidarity. Keenly aware of the environmental destruction caused by industrial society, they seek a sustainable relationship with nature. Arts and crafts flourish again, and people find joy in doing things with their own hands.

However, technology is conspicuously absent from Morris's account, and his vision is often described as pastoral. Although Morris does mention the existence of 'immensely improved machinery' (Ibid.: 127), it seems that most work is done by hand. However, it would be incorrect to attribute an anti-technological position to Morris; instead, we must see him as a writer concerned with 'alternative technology' (Coleman 1991: 28). Morris refused to speculate about future technology, being more concerned with describing the basic normative principles regulating the life of a good society, principles that should be observed when forming its technological basis. Given more than a hundred years of technological progress and taking into account the possibility of transformed, alternative technology, the question should be raised again: What kind of technologies would be developed by the free and equal people of the epoch of rest?

References

Bastani, A. (2019), *Fully Automated Luxury Communism: A Manifesto*, New York and London: Verso.

Bellamy, J. ([1888] 2009), *Looking Backward: 2000 1887*, Oxford: Oxford University Press.

Borgman, A. (1984), *Technology and the Character of Modern Life: A Philosophical Inquiry*, Chicago, IL and London: The University of Chicago Press.

Bridle, J. (2018), *New Dark Age: Technology and the End of the Future*, New York and London: Verso.

Cohen, G. A. (1978), *Karl Mar's Theory of History: A Defence*, Oxford: Clarendon Press.

Coleman, R. (1991), 'Design and Technology in Nowhere', *Journal of William Morris Studies*, 9 (2): 28–39.

Danaher, J. (2019), *Automation and Utopia: Human Flourishing in a World without Work*, Cambridge, MA and London: Harvard University Press.

Ellul, J. (1964), *The Technological Society*, New York: Vintage Books.

Feenberg, A. (1996), 'Marcuse or Habermas: Two Critiques of Technology', *Inquiry*, 39 (1): 45–70.

Feenberg, A. (2002), *Transforming Technology: A Critical Theory Revisited*, Oxford: Oxford University Press.

Habermas, J. (1970), *Towards a Rational Society: Student Protest, Science and Politics*, Boston, MA: Beacon Press.

Heidegger, M. (1977), *The Question Concerning Technology and Other Essays*, New York and London: Garland Publishing.

Jones, P. (2021), *Work without the Worker: Labour in the Age of Platform Capitalism*, London and New York: Verso.

Malm, A. (2016), *Fossil Capital: The Rise of Steam Power and the Roots of Global Warming*, New York and London: Verso.

Marcuse, H. (1969), *An Essay on Liberation*, Boston, MA: Beacon Press.

Marx, K. (1859), *Preface to A Contribution of the Critique of Political Economy*. https://www.marxists.org/archive/marx/works/1859/critique-pol-economy/preface.htm (accessed 12 March 2024).

Marx, K. (1988), *Economic Manuscripts of 1861–1863*. In Karl Marx, Friedrich Engels, *Collected Works*, vol. 30, Moscow: Progress Publishers.

Marx, K. (1990), *Capital*, vol. 1, London: Penguin Classics.

Mason, P. (2015), *PostCapitalism: A Guide to Our Future*, London: Allen Lane.

Mason, P. 2019. *Clear Bright Future: A Radical Defence of the Human Being*, London: Allen Lane.

Morris, W. (2004), *News from Nowhere and Other Writings*, London: Penguin Books.

Saito, K. (2023), *Marx in the Anthropocene: Towards the Idea of Degrowth Communism*, Cambridge: Cambridge University Press.

Srnicek, N. and Williams, A. (2013), *#Accelerate: Manifesto for an Accelerationist Politics*. https://syntheticedifice.files.wordpress.com/2013/06/accelerate.pdf (accessed 12 March 2024).

Srnicek, N. and Williams, A. (2016), *Inventing the Future: Postcapitalism and a World without Work*, London; New York: Verso.

Index

Adorno, Theodor W. 8, 108
algorithm (algorithmic) 9, 12, 30, 31, 33, 63, 70, 71–85, 133, 192, 196
alienation 3, 7–9, 12, 26, 27, 38, 42, 69, 109–11, 113–17, 119, 121, 129, 130, 132–3, 136, 142–3, 145–8, 150, 153, 155, 156, 160, 162, 166, 178, 181, 195
American Federation of Labor 42
Aristotle 1, 4, 5, 6, 9, 13–15, 17, 21–4, 27–8, 36–7, 41, 42, 44–6, 110, 111–14, 118–25, 126, 208–9
Artificial Intelligence (AI) 2, 12, 23, 24, 29–35, 36, 38, 63, 74, 129, 130–1, 135–6, 138, 145–6, 148–9, 154, 182, 187, 196
  AI as a tool 2, 6, 15, 20–21, 24, 30
  Artificial General Intelligence (AGI) 30, 34
  GOFAI 31
  machine learning (ML) 31, 131, 133, 134, 136, 192
  AI industry 6, 11, 12, 28–9
  political economy of AI 12, 28–32, 33, 35
  risks of AI 34–5, 130
  intelligence 8, 29, 30, 34, 35, 36, 130, 131, 132, 133, 135, 136, 137, 138, 141, 142, 148, 153, 156

automation 2, 3, 6, 9, 11, 13, 25, 26, 33, 34, 37, 38, 54, 71, 73, 110, 111, 119–21, 123, 125, 155, 159, 162, 166, 181, 182, 190, 192, 196, 200

Baird, John Logie 56
Bastani, Aaron 3, 191
Bellamy, Edward 3, 9, 209, 210
Berle, Adolf 43
Bletchley Declaration 129–30
Braverman, Harry 7, 32, 43–6, 49, 51, 54
British Broadcasting Corporation (BBC) 52, 56–7
Bogdanov, Alexander 162–3, 170–1, 173, 176–81
  Red Star 170–1, 176–8, 180
Bolshevism, Bolshevik 8, 163, 165, 170, 171, 174–80
Borgmann, Albert 194–5, 197, 207–8
Bridle, James 148–9, 195–7
Bostrom, Nick 3, 38, 130
bureaucracy 48, 53, 73
Burnham, James 167–8
  The Managerial Revolution 168

Castoriadis, Cornelius 20, 173
ChatGPT 2, 11, 131–7, 140, 156
Christensen, Clay 59–60

Index

communication 54, 55, 71–3, 79, 144, 154
consumer 72, 74–5, 79, 83, 93, 95, 144
consumption 94
control 112, 115, 117, 153, 167, 174–6, 189, 191, 194
Cummins Engine Company 52

Danaher, John 37, 90, 159, 192
democracy (democratic) 3, 6, 28, 34, 154, 167, 173, 177, 191, 206
   workplace 173
dependence 68, 73, 75, 80, 147
deskilling 7, 43, 52, 54, 207
digitization 63
dystopia, dystopianism 2, 160–3, 165, 178, 181

efficiency 64, 71, 166, 174, 179, 193
Ellul, Jacques 193–4
embodied being, embodiment 132, 153–4
Engels, Friedrich 14, 17, 20, 21, 35, 36, 94
essentialism 143–4
excellence 5, 24, 26, 28–9, 33–4, 37, 41–2, 46, 50–2, 64–6, 80–5, 90, 95, 100, 102–5, 178
   standards of excellence 34, 37, 46, 52, 95, 102

failure 141, 151
Feenberg, Andrew 204–7
Fleming, Peter 37, 90
flourishing 4–8, 20, 22, 33–4, 64, 67–9, 105, 110, 118, 123, 143, 153–4, 193, 205, 208
Ford, Henry 43, 50, 90, 165, 174
frames of finitude 141–2, 147
functionalism 137–8

good/s 28, 37, 42, 46, 132, 148–9, 154
good work 66, 68, 82, 90, 97, 106
goods of effectiveness 66, 81
goods of excellence 65
external goods 7–8, 95, 99, 100–1
internal goods 37, 45, 65, 83, 97, 101, 106
Gastev, Aleksei 175–9
Gorz, André 91, 93–4, 96

Habermas, Jürgen 205–6
Hardt, Michael 29, 32
Hegel, Georg Wilhelm Friedrich 42, 181, 121
Heidegger, Martin 2, 69, 193, 195
Huxley, Aldous 3, 161–2, 165–8, 171, 178
   Brave New World 161, 167–8

institutions 7, 34, 38, 45, 48, 53–4, 60, 65–6, 81, 83, 101–2
intellectual property 60

Jones, Phil 35, 192
justice 48, 77, 90, 149, 152–3, 174, 193

Kant, Immanuel 42, 51, 113, 121
Keynes, John Maynard 5–7, 91–3, 98, 103, 105
Kollontai, Alexandra 173

labour 6, 12, 14, 16, 21–5, 65, 67–9, 71, 76, 78, 90, 92, 115, 117, 119–21, 146–7, 155, 174–6, 181, 191, 201–2
   alienated/estranged labour 110, 112–14
   non-alienated labour 20–8, 112

post-work 7, 25–6, 34, 37, 104, 156, 188, 190–2, 199, 209
wage-labour 27, 116
slavery (slaves) 26–7, 36, 41, 52, 164
Lawson, Clive 111
life-capacities 143–5, 154
Lenin, Vladimir Ilyich 162–3, 169, 170–8, 180–1
Lumiere brothers 56
Luther, Martin 55

machinery 110, 119–20, 160, 164, 162, 166–7, 170, 177, 178, 181, 210
   machine society 160, 162–3, 166–7, 169–70, 173, 176, 181
MacIntyre, Alasdair 4–5, 7, 13, 14, 24, 37, 38, 42, 44–55, 59–60, 63–70, 80–2, 85, 90, 92, 94–103
management 7–8, 37, 42–5, 52–3, 57–9, 63–4, 66–7, 70–1, 73–5, 77, 79–80, 83–4, 96, 174
managerialism 7, 167–8, 173, 180
manipulation 44, 48, 49, 67, 77
   manipulative relationships 84
Malevich, Kazimir 2
Malm, Andreas 202–4
Mason, Paul 3, 25, 190–1
Marcuse, Herbert 8, 109–11, 117, 122–4, 125, 161, 204–5
Marx, Karl 1, 3–6, 8–9, 12–16, 19–22, 27, 35–6, 38–9, 44–5, 51, 54, 69, 94, 110–22, 124–6, 142–7, 159–63, 166, 177–82, 197–9, 201–2
   Capital 36, 44, 110, 114–16, 201
   Fragment on Machines 22, 162, 181
   historical materialism 5–6, 12–20

German Ideology 14, 17, 20, 94
Paris Manuscripts 8, 162
species-being 69, 112–13, 115–16, 118, 124, 142, 145–6
Mazzucato, Mariana 34
McCarthy, John 29
McLuhan, Marshall 55, 59, 62
Mills, C. Wright 44
Moore, Mark 57
More, Thomas 18–19
Morozov, Evgeny 31–2
Morris, William 9, 84, 210
Murray, Patrick 122

Negri, Antonio 29, 32
needs 5–6, 34, 37, 103, 131, 143
   criterion / transformation of needs 13–14, 21, 144
Nicomachus 41–2
Nietzsche, Friedrich 42, 49–50
Nilsson, Nils John 29, 30

Ollman, Bertell 111
Orwell, George 161–71, 167, 178
   Nineteen Eighty-Four 161
   The Road to Wigan Pier 164–5, 170

platform 31–33, 35, 71–2, 74–9, 83–4, 189, 192
Popper, Karl Raimund 16
practice/s 5–8, 24, 28, 34, 36, 37, 38, 42, 45–8, 52, 55, 59–60, 65–6, 69, 72, 80, 82, 90, 95–105, 143, 148, 151, 164, 193–5
   artistic practice 152
Puttnam, David 56

rational deliberation 33, 80
Rawls, John 47–8, 207
recognition 7–8, 12, 28, 38, 89, 90, 98–106, 178

Reith, John 57
resistance 19, 53, 76, 206
Rifkin, Jeremy 38, 91
Roosevelt, Franklin Delano 43

Saito, Kohei 202
Schiller, Dan 31
Schuler, Jeanne 122
science fiction 130, 160–1, 163, 165, 170–1, 181
Smith, Adam 19
Soviet Union 51, 164, 167, 169–70
Spotify 83
Srnicek, Nick 3, 26, 29, 37, 189–91
Steinhoff, Jame 29, 30–2, 156
Stites, Richard 170–1, 174–81
  Revolutionary Dreams 170
suffering 91, 147
  suffering and human life-value 147
super-intelligence 132, 148
Sweezy, Paul 44, 54

Taylor, Frederick Winslow 54, 173–4, 176, 178
  Taylorism 7, 32, 43, 50, 54, 73, 173–4, 176, 179–80

technocracy 168, 171, 173, 175, 178–80
technotopia, technotopians 132, 146, 149, 150, 153, 154
Thompson, Edward Palmer 18, 42

Uber 71–2, 74–5
utopia, utopianism 8, 19, 34, 161–3, 165–6

Varoufakis, Yanis 34
virtue 41, 47–8, 102–3

Weber, Max 109
Weeks, Kathi 37, 90
Wendling, Amy E. 3, 111, 159
Wells, Herbert George 3, 160, 163, 165–6, 168, 171, 172
Williams, Alex 3, 26, 29, 38, 189–91
Wittgenstein, Ludwig 35, 47–8

Zamyatin, Yevgeny 3, 161–2, 168–9, 171–2, 176, 178, 180
  We 3, 161, 169, 171–2, 178, 180
Zerilli, John 29
Zuboff, Shoshana 31